THE DAM BUSTERS

THE WAR-TIME LEADERS OF 617 SQUADRON

Wing Commander Guy Gibson, V.C., D.S.O. and Bar, D.F.C. and Bar

Group Captain Leonard Cheshire, V.C., D.S.O. and 2 Bars, D.F.C.

Wing Commander H. B. (Micky) Martin, D.S.O. and Bar., D.F.C. and 2 Bars, A.F.C.

Wing Commander J. B. Tait, D.S.O. and 3 Bars, D.F.C. and Bar

Air Commodore J. E. Fauquier, D.S.O. and 2 Bars, D.F.C.

THE
DAM BUSTERS

by
PAUL BRICKHILL

Cadet Edition

THE CHILDREN'S BOOK CLUB
121 CHARING CROSS ROAD
LONDON W.C.2

© PAUL BRICKHILL

CADET EDITION 1958

This edition by arrangement with Evans Brothers Ltd.

Printed in Great Britain by
Cox & Wyman Ltd., London, Fakenham and Reading

To the men living and dead
who did these things

CONTENTS

CHAPTER   PAGE

I. A WEAPON IS CONCEIVED 9

II. —AND REJECTED 17

III. THE GREEN LIGHT 28

IV. A SQUADRON IS BORN 36

V. OVER THE HURDLES 45

VI. TAKE-OFF 56

VII. ATTACK 69

VIII. THE WRITHING LAKE 80

IX. THE BLACKEST HOUR 92

X. SNIPER SQUADRON 109

XI. DIRECT HIT 117

XII. GALLANT FAILURE 123

XIII. THE MOSQUITO PLAN 134

XIV. THE UNAPPEASING OF MUNICH . . . 140

XV. EARTHQUAKE BOMB 151

XVI. SMASHING THE SECRET WEAPON . . . 159

XVII. VICTORIA CROSS 169

XVIII. THE NAKED BATTLESHIP 178

XIX. BACK FROM THE DEAD 182

XX. "GRAND SLAM" 186

EPILOGUE 191

LIST OF ILLUSTRATIONS

THE WAR-TIME LEADERS OF 617 SQUADRON . *Frontispiece*

facing page

GIBSON AND HIS CREW CLIMBING INTO G FOR GEORGE . . 64

THE EDER DAM BREACHED 64

GIBSON'S CREW TELL THEIR STORY AT DE-BRIEFING . . 65

THE MOEHNE DAM BREACHED 65

THE MOMENT IN WHICH H.M. KING GEORGE VI SELECTED
617 SQUADRON'S BADGE 80

THE MOMENT AT WHICH CHESHIRE DROPPED INCENDIARY
MARKERS ON THE FACTORY AT LIMOGES 81

THE REMARKABLE BOMBING OF THE MICHELIN FACTORY . 81

THE DIRECT HIT ON THE SAUMUR TUNNEL 128

BARNES WALLIS 129

THE *Tirpitz* LYING CAPSIZED IN TROMSO FIORD . . . 144

A TEN-TON "GRAND SLAM" 145

THE BIELEFELD VIADUCT 145

*For permission to reproduce the photographs in this book the author
and publishers are indebted to the Imperial War Museum.*

CHAPTER I

A WEAPON IS CONCEIVED

THE day before the war started Barnes Wallis drove for five
hours back to Vickers' works at Weybridge, leaving his
wife and family in the quiet Dorset bay where they had pitched
tents for a holiday. He had that morning reluctantly decided
that war was not only inevitable but imminent, and he was
going to be needed at his drawing-board.

Wallis did not look like a man who was going to have much
influence on the war. At 53 his face was unlined and com-
posed, the skin smooth and pink and the eyes behind the horn-
rimmed glasses mild and grey; crisp white hair like a woolly
cap enhanced the effect of benevolence. Many people who
stood in his way in the next three years were deceived by this.

He spent the last night of peace alone in his house near
Effingham, and in the morning, like most people, listened to
the oddly inspiring speech of Chamberlain's. Afterwards he
sat in silence and misery.

One thought had been haunting him since the previous
morning's decision: what could he, as an aircraft designer
and engineer, do to shorten the war? The thought stayed
with him for a long time and through remarkable events
before it was honourably discharged.

He had been designing for Vickers since before the first
world war. In the twenties he designed the R.100, the most
successful British dirigible. In the thirties he invented the
geodetic form of aircraft construction and, using this, designed
the Wellesley which captured the world's non-stop distance
record, and the Wellington, which was the mainstay of Bomber
Command for the first three years of the war.

9

Vickers' works, nestled in the baked perimeter of the old Brooklands motor-racing track, was turning out Wellingtons as fast as it could, and Wallis was designing its proposed successor, the Warwick. At this time he was on the design of the Warwick's tailplane, which was being troublesome. Clearly any additional work would have to be done in his own spare time and there was, also quite clearly, not going to be much spare time.

Bombers and bombs were the directions in which he was most qualified to help. Bombs, particularly, seemed a fruitful field. He knew something about R.A.F. bombs, their size, shape, weight and so on; the knowledge had been essential when he was designing the Wellington, so that it could carry the required bombs over the required distance. It was not knowledge which, in Wallis, inspired complacency. The heaviest bomb was only 500 lb., and aiming was so unpredictable that the Air Force was forced to indulge in stick bombing—you dropped them one after another in the pious hope that one would hit the target. One hoped then that it would go off. Too many didn't.

R.A.F. bombs, too, were old, very old. Nearly all were stocks hoarded from 1919. There had been an attempt in 1921 to design a better bomb, and in 1938 they actually started to produce them, but in 1940 there were still very few of them. Both new bombs and old were filled with a mediocre explosive called amatol (and only 25 per cent of the weight consisted of explosive). There *was* a far better explosive called RDX, but production of that had been stopped in 1937. (It was not till 1942 that the R.A.F. was able to use RDX-filled bombs.) Meantime Luftwaffe bombs contained a much more powerful explosive than amatol—and half the weight of the German bomb was explosive.

Wallis knew there had been an attempt in 1926 to make 1,000-lb. bombs for the R.A.F. but they never even got to the testing stage. The Treasury was against them; the Air Staff thought they would never need a bomb larger than 500 lb., and anyway Air Force planes were designed to carry 500-pounders. Not till 1939 did the Air Staff begin to think seriously again of the 1,000-pounder, and six months *after* the war started they placed an order for some.

These shortcomings were not so obvious then, particularly as all air forces favoured small bombs designed to attack surface targets. The blast of bigger bombs was curiously local against buildings, and a lot of little bombs seemed better than an equal weight of larger ones. Even larger bombs needed a direct hit to cause much damage and there was more chance of a direct hit with a lot of little bombs.

To Wallis's methodically logical mind there was a serious flaw to all this. Factories and transport could be dispersed; in fact *were* dispersed all over Germany. Bombing (vintage 1939) would not damage enough factories to make much difference.

He started wondering *where* and *how* bombing could hurt Germany most. If one could not hit the dispersed war effort perhaps there were key points. Perhaps the sources of the effort. And here the probing mind was fastening on a new principle.

The sources of Germany's effort, in war or peace, lay in power. Not political power, but physical power! Great sources of energy too massive to move or hide—coal mines, oil dumps and wells, and "white coal"—hydro-electric power from dams. Without them there could be no production and no transport. No weapons. No war.

But they were too massive to dent by existing bombs. One might as well kick them with a dancing pump! The next step—in theory anyway—was easy. Bigger bombs. Much bigger!

But that meant bigger aircraft; much bigger than existing ones. All right then—bigger aircraft too.

That was the start of it. It sounds simple but it was against the tenets of the experts of every air force in the world.

*　　　*　　　*

Wallis started calculating and found the blast of bigger bombs *was* puny against steadfast targets like coal mines, buried oil and dams. Particularly dams, ramparts of ferro-concrete anchored in the earth.

Then perhaps a new *type* of bomb. But there Wallis did not know enough about bombs and the logic stopped short.

The war was a few weeks old when the dogged scientist dived into engineering and scientific libraries and at lunch-times, when he pushed the problem of the Warwick's tail-plane aside for an hour or so, he sent out for sandwiches, stayed at his desk and started to learn about bombs. At night at home he did the same, absorbed and lost to his family for hours. As the hard winter of 1939 arrived he progressed to the study of the sources of power.

Coal mines! Impossible to collapse the galleries and tunnels hundreds of feet underground. Possible, he decided, that a heavy bomb might collapse the winding shaft so that the lift would not work. No lift. No work. No coal. But that could soon be repaired.

Oil! Rumanian oil fields were too far for existing bombers, but a possibility for a future bomber. Germany's synthetic refineries were massive and well defended; perhaps a target for bigger bombers.

Dams! Three German dams stood out—the Moehne, the Eder and the Sorpe. All in the Ruhr, they accounted for nearly all the water supply to that monstrous arsenal. Wallis knew that the German method needed eight tons of water to produce a ton of steel. The possibilities were intriguing.

The Moehne dammed Moehne Lake where the Heve flowed into the Ruhr River, maintaining the level so that barges with coal and steel and tanks could go to and from the foundries. Moehne Lake held 134 million tons of water. The Eder dammed the Eder River in Eder Lake, 212 million tons of water. It controlled the level of Germany's second most important waterway, the Mittelland Canal. Even Kassel, forty miles away, got its water from the Eder. The

Sorpe dammed another tributary of the Ruhr River in Sorpe Lake.

The Moehne was 112 feet thick at the base, 130 feet high and 25 feet thick at the top where a roadway ran; the Eder was even bigger. Wallis acknowledged that they were formidable. A 500-lb. bomb would hardly scratch the concrete. No less formidable the Sorpe, an earth dam, two sloping mounds of earth sealed and buttressed in the centre by a core of concrete.

In an engineering library Wallis unearthed accounts of their construction compiled by the proud engineers who had built them and found it hard to discipline his excitement as he read what the effects of breaching the dams could be.

It would not merely destroy hydro-electric power and deprive foundries of essential water, but affect other war factories which needed water for their processes. Disrupting them might cause a dozen critical bottlenecks in the completion of tanks, locomotives, guns, aircraft—almost anything one cared to name. It would deprive the populace of water too, which was no cause for joy in a gentle soul like Wallis but would at least induce in them a lessening of zest for the war.

There was still more to it. Breaches in the dams would send enormous floods ripping down the valleys, tearing away roads, bridges and railway lines, smashing factories and houses, so that some factories, rather than be deprived of water, would receive somewhat too much.

All this was fine, Wallis thought . . . logical ideas; but again one big flaw. The dams were so colossal that bombs twenty times bigger than existing ones were not going to hurt them.

His figures showed that when a 1,000-pounder exploded the charge expanded as a gas bubble, but at the end the bubble was only 20 feet across. A lot of damage was done beyond this 10-foot radius, however, by flying fragments, by blast and by the pressure pulse, or "shock wave." Wallis well remembered the pedantic description of shockwaves . . . "there is no motion of the transmitting medium other than the usual oscillation of particles to and fro about their position of rest as the wave passes through them." Thin air gave scope to flying fragments and blast but the shock wave soon dissipated. It would vibrate a structure, but not enough. To be destructive, shock waves had to travel through a more solid medium than air. And somewhere in Wallis's brain a little cell awoke and stirred restlessly, an old memory, locked up and almost forgotten. He felt there was something he knew about shock waves that he should remember, tried to think what it was—it was a long time ago—but the harder he tried the farther it receded. It was only when he put it out of his mind that it sneaked insidiously back to him again.

It was something he had read, something about concrete. And then it hit him. Waterloo Bridge! Concrete piles being driven into the bed of the Thames! That was years ago. The piles had kept shattering mysteriously and there had been an investigation. He started searching his bookcases and in a quarter of an hour had found it, an article in a 1935 journal of the Institution of Civil Engineers. The great drop-hammers had been slamming the piles into the river-bed and the tops of the piles had been exploding upwards.

Investigation narrowed the cause to the shock waves. The sudden blows sent shock waves shivering down the piles; at the bottom they met the blunt resistance of the clay and bounced back up the pile at something like 15,000 feet a second, reaching the top just after the hammer had bounced off, so there was nothing to rebound from again and they passed out and away, and in their wake you got a tension after the compression. A sort of crush and then a sharp stretch, almost in the same moment; enough to make a structure split—to shatter it.

Concrete, the article concluded sagely, well resisted compression but poorly withstood tension. Wallis docketed the fact in his mind, thinking of dams.

You needed a solid medium to get destructive shock waves! Of course, if you could bury a bomb *deep* in . . . But you couldn't slice a big bomb into ferro-concrete. No, but you might be able to inject it deep into some less solid medium before it exploded. You'd get the shock waves then. The expanding gas effects would be greater too; tamped by the encircling solids they would have to burst their way out.

He was aware that bombs and shells often buried themselves 3 or 4 feet in the ground before exploding, but that was so shallow the explosion forced its way easily to the top, causing a small crater, and the shock waves dissipated into the air. It was less effective than a surface explosion because the blast and shock waves went straight up instead of outwards.

But if you could *lock* the explosion underground so it could not break out you would get a sort of seismic disturbance . . . an earthquake! An earthquake bomb!

The idea shaped in his mind while he was sitting in a deep chair in his home at Effingham, an unspectacular setting for the birth of something so powerful.

But how to sink a bomb deeply into a resisting medium? You could not put one deep into a concrete dam. But a dam is set in water!

Water! It might not transmit a shock wave as well as earth but it would do so better than air. The tamping effect of water would produce a concentrated explosion and carry the "shock" punch. Wallis was starting to feel he might be getting somewhere.

And how about sinking the bomb in earth? A schoolboy knew the two principles. The heavier the bomb, the more power and speed it developed in falling. Wallis had learned the classic example in school. Drop a mouse down a well and at the bottom it will be able to get up and run. Drop a horse down and the horse will probably burst. Because it was heavier it would hit *harder*. And the *farther* it fell, the *faster* it would fall!

So there it was: a bomb as heavy as possible (and as slim as possible) dropped from as high as possible.

Wallis looked up more books, studied the propagation of

shock waves in soil, the effects of underground explosions at depth, and even found pages on the penetrative powers into soils of shells and light bombs. There was a piece about an enormous land mine exploded under a German-held hill at Messines Ridge in World War I. A colossal charge sent shock waves ripping into the earth, the hill was destroyed and the shock was felt in Cassell—30 miles away.

Wallis pulled out a pad and pencil and worked for a week, covering sheets with calculations, equations, formulæ—and came up with a preliminary theoretical answer. A 10-ton bomb, with 7 tons of explosive in an ærodynamically-designed case of special steel, dropped from 40,000 feet, would reach a speed of 1,440 feet per second, or 982 m.p.h.—well over the speed of sound. At that rate it should penetrate an average soil to a depth of 135 feet.

A charge of that size should theoretically "camouflet" (not break the surface) at a depth of 130 feet. What it *would* do was cause a violent earthquake movement on the surface resulting in a hump forming.

"Such earth movements," said a learned paper, "are capable of doing much damage at great distances."

It looked as though Wallis had found his answer. Or part of it.

CHAPTER II

—AND REJECTED

H E worked out theoretical effects, more pages of figures, and decided there was a chance that a 10-ton bomb exploding deep in water by a dam wall would punch out a hole a hundred feet across.

Supposing the bomb did not go as deeply into the earth as the figures predicted? Wallis worked out the effects of a 10-tonner exploding about 40 feet deep. In theory it would throw out the staggering amount of 12,000 tons of earth, leaving a crater 70 feet deep, with lips 250 feet across. He worked out the circumference of the crater and from that the maximum number of men and machines that could gather round the edges. Working day and night they could not fill it in under fourteen days! Supposing one such bomb was dropped accurately in a marshalling yard! Or on a vital railway or canal or road where ground contours prohibited a detour!

Wallis did not get too excited. No bomber in the world would carry a 10-ton bomb. Or for that matter even a 5-ton bomb far enough to get it to a target.

Back to pencil and paper. He knew the limitations of aircraft design in 1940 and in a couple of weeks he knew it was possible to build a 50-ton bomber to carry a 10-ton bomb 4,000 miles at 320 m.p.h. and a height of 45,000 feet. He drew up rough specifications and christened it the "Victory Bomber."

And the aiming of bombs—notoriously hit and miss, mostly miss. Wallis found that increasing height did not greatly increase the problems and estimated that new bomb sights being developed and special training could put the bombs near enough to a target to destroy it.

That was the beauty of this 10-ton bomb. It should not have to be a direct hit! The earthquake shock would be so great that a near miss should shake a target to destruction. And another thing—a big bomb exploding 130 feet deep would not crater the surface but cause a huge subterranean cavern. Put such a bomb alongside a bridge or viaduct, and if the shock wave did not shake it to pieces the cavern underneath would knock its support away. An opening trapdoor—a hangman's drop! The bridge would collapse into it.

There was one other possibility in it—perhaps the greatest of all. A few such bombs, accurately aimed, might shatter the roots of a nation's war effort. That could mean the end of the dreadful "Guernica" carpet bombing, which saturated an area with bombs so limited in effect that the area had to be saturated to make their use militarily worth while. Wiping out cities and civilians at the same time!

Wallis spent weeks setting it all out on paper and took it to people he knew in the R.A.F. and the Ministry of Aircraft Production. It was Dunkirk time. A potent new weapon had never been better timed.

Wallis's paper on the "earthquake bomb" roused three main emotions in officials: (1) Lukewarm interest. (2) Incomprehension. (3) Tactful derision.

One man understood and did what he could: Arthur Tedder, a quiet, intensely likeable man smoking a pipe, chained to a desk in Whitehall. But he was only an air vice-marshal then and did not have the influence he acquired later. He brought the bomb and Victory Bomber to the attention of several people in high places but the only result seemed to be a ubiquitous manifestation of courteous but implacable inactivity. Every machine in the country was working overtime on other vital things and the ambitious and excellent four-engined bomber project was just getting under way. It was a fair assumption that it might be disastrous to dislocate that in favour of the Victory Bomber, which would inevitably take much longer to develop. That automatically prejudiced the shock-wave bomb, because there was therefore no aircraft in sight which could drop it from Wallis's prescribed height of 40,000 feet. The new bombers would probably not be able to lift it or, if they could, to carry it far enough to drop it from higher than 20,000 feet, which was not likely to be enough.

And then on July 19, out of the blue, Wallis got an urgent summons to see Lord Beaverbrook, the bright-eyed firecracker who was Minister for Aircraft Production. With "The Beaver" interested anything could happen, and probably at speed. He caught the first train to London, cooled his heels a few minutes in an ante-room and then the big door opened and a young man said:

"Lord Beaverbrook will see you now, sir."

Wallis jumped up, cuddling his calculations under his arm, and crossed the threshold, nervous with anticipation; and there was the little man with the wide, mobile mouth, sitting slightly hunched in his chair. It was the speed with which things happened that shook Wallis as much as the things themselves. No gracious, measured preliminaries. He was still in the middle of the floor, walking, when the little man barked:

"What's this about a ten-ton bomb?"

Wallis told him as concisely as he could; difficult for a scientist, who always feels compelled to go into technicalities, but he kept it short and lucid and Beaverbrook was interested.

"You know how short we are of stuff," he said. "This thing's only a theory. We'd have to stop work on other vital things to make it and then it might be a flop."

"It won't be that," Wallis said stubbornly.

"We'd still have to stop work on other things."

"It will be worth it."

"Take too long, wouldn't it?" said "The Beaver." "A ten-ton bomb and a bomber twice the size of anything else sounds like something in the distant future."

"We can do it in stages, sir," Wallis said. "I've got drawings for two-ton and six-ton bombs on the same principle. My

Wellingtons can carry the two-tonner all right. The new four-engined ones can carry the six-tonner. They'll be operating in a year."

"Well, I'll see my experts about it," Beaverbrook said. "If it's going to mean diverting too much effort I don't like your chances."

Little seemed to happen for a while but behind the scenes things were moving in a ponderous government way. Little snippets filtered through to Wallis, particularly from that astute ally, Arthur Tedder. Nothing much; just that So-and-so had consented to look into the idea and that So-and-so had expressed mild interest. Wallis thought the prospects were still favourable. Sir Charles Craven, managing director of Vickers, was sympathetic and felt confident enough on November 1 to write to Beaverbrook suggesting he give permission to go ahead on both 10-ton bomb and Victory Bomber.

Then Tedder was posted to take over the R.A.F. in the Middle East and Wallis had lost his keenest supporter in the sacred and essential precincts of Whitehall. It was soon after that Craven sent for him.

"I'm afraid I haven't very encouraging news for you," Craven said as kindly as he could. "Air Council seem too wary of big bombs. They still believe stick bombing is necessary."

"But can't they *see* what a really big bomb would do?" Wallis said pleadingly.

"Apparently not. They say that from experience they would rather drop four 250-pound bombs than a thousand-pounder. Much less a 22,000-pounder."

"Could they understand my calculations, sir?"

Craven did not comment on their understanding. He said diplomatically that he doubted whether the members would have the *time* to go individually through all the calculations. Which was probably true. And then gently: "They say that anyone who thinks of ten-ton bombs is mad."

Wallis went back to Weybridge in anger, but in the morning

the anger had mostly gone and in its place was outraged stubbornness. He started writing a treatise on his 10-ton bomb and called it "A note on a method of attacking the Axis Powers," the kind of obscure title so favoured by scientists; the word "note" being particularly misleading, as such things are often as long as a book.

Wallis's was. He started by outlining his theory of crippling an enemy by destroying the sources of energy, and went on to discuss in exhaustive detail the physical qualities of the targets, shock waves, blast, penetration, bomb design, aircraft design, charge/weight ratios, aiming problems, possible effects, repair potentialities, backed up with pages of graphs and formulæ and equations. It was a *tour de force*, explaining step by step so lucidly that a layman could follow it if he took the mathematics for granted.

The "note" took Wallis several months, and then he had it roneoed and bound and posted copies to seventy influential men in science, politics and the services.

Results were not long coming. A secret service man called on him with a copy of the "note" under his arm.

"Did you send this to Mr.——?" he asked.

"Yes," Wallis said. "Why?"

"I'm afraid you shouldn't have done so, Mr. Wallis."

"Why?"

"It's very secret stuff. This sort of thing must be handled very carefully and only reach authorised persons. Mr.—— was very surprised when this arrived in the post. We were concerned too. I quite realise you didn't mean to be . . ."

"I sent out seventy of them," Wallis said calmly, and the Secret Service was appalled.

"Seventy!" he said. "*Seventy!* Who? To whom? But you shouldn't have. This is vital and very secret!"

"Is it?" said Wallis mildly. "When I showed it to the authorised persons they said I was mad. I'm supposed to be a crackpot and this is regarded by authorised persons as fiddle-faddle."

The secret service man said, "Oh!" He asked for the names

of the seventy. Wallis read them out and the secret service man, who seemed a little uncertain of his ground, went back to London to investigate further.

He appeared again a couple of days later.

"Well, it's all right," he said, "this time. We've decided that as so many were sent out so openly it's actually rather a good form of security. No one will dream it's all so secret. But please don't do it again."

Wallis bowed gravely. "I hope it will not be necessary again," he said and the incident was closed.

A few days later there was another result. A copy had reached a Group Captain Winterbotham, who had an office in the City and was used to dealing with unorthodox aspects of the war. He had found it convincing, called on Wallis, and Wallis explained more fully. Winterbotham caught some of his enthusiasm. He knew Sir Henry Tizard, who was scientific adviser to the Ministry of Aircraft Production, and drew his special attention to Wallis's paper.

Tizard read it carefully; as a scientist he could follow the intricate calculations. He went down to see Wallis at Weybridge and was impressed.

"I'd better form a committee to study this more fully," he said. "It would have to have pretty solid backing from expert opinion. You'll understand, I know. It would divert effort from other important things if we were to go ahead with it and we've got to be reasonably sure it would be worth while."

"Of course," Wallis said. He felt like singing.

Not long after, Wallis met the committee. At the head was Dr. Pye, Director of Scientific Research at the Ministry of Supply, and the others were scientists too. Wallis explained his ideas and described the probable effect on Germany's war industries if the dams were breached. There was only one really worthwhile time of the year to breach them, and that was in May, when the storage lakes were full after the winter thaw and spring rains, and before the sluice gates were opened to water the country and canals for summer. Then you would get the greatest floods, the most serious loss of water and power. Dr. Pye said the committee would be a few days considering.

A week later Wallis faced the committee to hear their findings. His worst fears were soon over; the report was favourable, but, as they read on, a little disappointingly so. They thought that the dams showed possibilities and the upshot was another committee. This one focused the aim more definitely; it was to be called "The Air Attack on Dams Committee."

The members were again scientists and engineers and in a mood to be interested in something new because even German bombs, though they were more efficient than R.A.F. bombs and killed thousands of civilians, had demonstrated the limitations of small bombs.

"With this big bomb," Wallis earnestly impressed on them, "you don't have to get a direct hit. I think a ten-ton bomb dropped fifty feet away stands a good chance of knocking a hole in a dam like the Moehne. A near miss like that ought to be simple enough to organise."

One of the members, Dr. Glanville, of the Road Research Laboratories at Harmondsworth, suggested building a model dam and testing the theories with scaled-down charges of explosive. Wallis accepted delightedly.

Over the next few months, whenever he could spare time from his arduous work at Vickers, Wallis helped Glanville design and painstakingly build a model dam one-fiftieth the size of the Moehne with tiny cubes of concrete, scale models of the huge masonry blocks in the real dam. The model was about 30 feet long, 33 inches high and up to 2 feet thick, a low wall arched between earthern banks, secluded from prying outside eyes in a walled garden.

They flooded the ground at one side to simulate the lake, and Wallis exploded a few ounces of gelignite under the surface 4 feet from the model to give the effect of a 10-tonner going off 200 feet away. There was a commotion on the water and a couple of patches of concrete flaked and chipped.

"Not so good there," Wallis said. "Let's try it closer."

He exploded more gelignite 3 feet from the dam, and there was a little more damage. He set off another charge 2 feet away and still found only minor chipping.

At a distance of 12 inches (representing a 10-tonner 50 feet from the dam) the gelignite caused a couple of cracks in the outer structure; but they were small cracks, not enough to harm the dam significantly. They tried several more charges but the cumulative effect was not encouraging.

Months had passed since the first hopeful meeting of the committee, and Wallis could see that their early co-operation was freezing. Glanville built another model, and Wallis tried bigger charges to see what *would* smash the models at a distance. One day a few extra ounces of gelignite a foot away sent a mushroom of water spraying over the wall round the garden and as the spume cleared they saw the water of the little lake gushing through the burst dam. Slabs of concrete had cracked and spilled out and there was the breach that Wallis had been wanting. He calculated the scaled-up charge which, dropped 50 feet away, would smash such a hole in the Moehne. The answer was something like 30,000 lb. of the new explosive RDX, and the gentle scientist did not need pencil and paper to estimate the significance.

Thirty thousand pounds was nearly 14 tons. That was the explosive alone. Add the weight of the thick case of special steel—another 40,000 odd lb. It meant a bomb weighing 70,000 lb.—over 30 tons, and the Victory Bomber, still only on paper and straining the limits of feasible aircraft construction, would carry only a 10-tonner.

The next meeting of the Air Attack on Dams Committee was in a fortnight and it required little thought to foresee it would be the last meeting.

Wallis would not give up.

Supposing, he thought, a bomb could be exploded *under water against* the dam wall. The shock wave punch would be much greater. So the explosive needed would be smaller. So would the bomb casing.

But how to get a big bomb in the exact spot—deep enough for the shock punch and pressed against the wall to make the most of it? Or, as it might require more than one bomb, how could you get them all in the exact spot? A torpedo? But the dams had heavy torpedo netting in front of them, and so torpedoes were out. You could drop a bomb from very low level for accuracy, but bombs don't simply "drop". Just after release they carry a lot of forward speed, giving them almost a horizontal trajectory for a while. If you dropped a bomb—even a whopper—from very low to get the accuracy it would simply skid off the water; so that was no good. If you dropped it high enough to enter the water cleanly, you only had about one chance in a thousand of putting it right in the exact spot.

Wallis probed at this problem for days and every time he probed he came slap up against the same old problem—the only way would be to drop something from very, very low and somehow make it stay where it was supposed to. But that seemed to be impossible. He remembered his last holiday with the youngsters just before the war began when they had been skipping stones across the smooth water of a little pond. How on earth, he thought, could one toss a stone low like that and stop it skipping. Drop any shape of bomb very low at a couple of hundred miles an hour and heaven knows where it would skip to. When dams are full there is practically no space between the level of the water and the top of the dam wall and in his wry imagination he visualised a series of grotesque bombs hurdling over the dam wall and flying harmlessly downstream. What a pity, he thought idly, that you couldn't make a torpedo do a bit of hurdling—over an anti-torpedo net for instance.

Hullo! That was an idea! If a bomb could hurdle a dam wall it could also hurdle an anti-torpedo net. Such nets were a good hundred yards away from dam walls to keep any explosions at arm's length. A bomb didn't have to keep skipping for ever. May be it could be so judged to skip the torpedo net and not skip the dam wall. Hang it all, why not? He felt sudden excitement surging inside him. There would probably be three or four feet of dam wall above the water. Supposing the skipping of the bomb were timed (if it could be done) so that it was slithering to a stop on the water as it reached the wall. Why then, the wall would stop it dead and it would simply sink into the water, by the wall, as deep as you like. You could have the fuse fixed with a hydrostatic trigger so that the bomb would go off when the water pressure reached the right amount. Set in for fifty feet down or a hundred and fifty feet down. Please yourself. Hang it, the more he thought about it the more he liked the idea, even if it did sound a bit odd.

Wallis went home, dragged a tub into the garden of his house at Effingham and filled it right to the top with water. Then he rigged up a catapult a few feet away just a few inches above the level of the water. A few feet on the other side of the tub he stretched a string between a couple of sticks so that the string was also just above the level of the water. Then he borrowed a marble from his young daughter, Elizabeth, and shot it from the catapult at the water. It skipped off and cleared the string by several inches. Elizabeth and the other children looked on, wondering what he was up to. Elizabeth brought the marble back and Wallis fired it again, this time with a little less tension on the rubber of the catapult. The marble zipped off the water and only just cleared the string. "Ah," thought Wallis, "that's it."

He and the youngsters spent the whole morning playing with the marbles and the water and the catapult and the string, trying different combinations of power and height while Wallis was finding out how much he could control the skip. To his deep joy he found out that with a regular shape and weight like a marble on smooth water he could control it quite well. At least well enough for it to be distinctly encouraging. But could he control several skips, which might be necessary? Aha, that remained to be seen. They went into lunch eventually, all thoroughly splashed. Wallis was very cheerful, and also, the children thought, very mysterious about it all.

Always sensitive to ridicule, Wallis told no one the details, not even his friend Mutt Summers, chief test pilot for Vickers and the man who had tested his old warhorse, the Wellington. Captain Summers was a hefty extrovert and not the type to take a freak idea seriously.

The day of the meeting of the Air Attack on Dams Committee Wallis went early to London, buttonholed the chairman, Dr. Pye, and privately explained his new theory, so earnestly that Pye did not laugh though he looked a little sideways.

"I'd rather you didn't tell the others yet," Wallis said. "They might think it a bit far-fetched."

"Yes," said Dr. Pye. "I see that. What do you want me to do?"

"Give me time to find out how much RDX will blow a hole in the Moehne Dam if it's pressed up against the wall."

Pye talked eloquently to the committee without giving Wallis's secret away. The members were reluctant when they heard the results of the last model's test and Wallis was like a cat on hot bricks till they consented to one more experiment.

Glanville built him a new model dam, and Wallis started with small charges, sinking them in the water and exploding them when they were lying against the slabs of concrete. The effect was shattering—literally. He smashed wall after wall seeking the smallest charge needed, and soon he knew that in a contact explosion tamped by water a tiny plug of a few ounces of gelignite blasted a satisfying hole through a concrete wall 6 inches thick. From that he calculated he would need only 6,000 lb. of RDX to breach the Moehne Dam. With his new idea he could cut the case weight down to a little over 3,000 lb., making the complete bomb about 9,500 lb. Less than 5 tons. The new four-engined Lancasters would carry that to the Ruhr without trouble.

CHAPTER III

THE GREEN LIGHT

Aᴿᴹᴇᴅ with sums and theories, Wallis faced the task of convincing officials in their brick and stone lairs along Whitehall and other influential thoroughfares that he could put his bomb in the exact spot. He called on Professor Patrick Blackett, director of an "operational research" branch, and Blackett, a spare, rather intense man, listened to his ideas, carefully examined the calculations, riffled them back into a neat pile and said quietly:

"We've been looking for this for two years."

Wallis was electrified.

"I'd like you to leave these with me for a while," Blackett said. "There are one or two people I know who would be interested."

Blackett moved fast. As soon as Wallis had left he went to see Sir Henry Tizard and told him what he had heard. Tizard also moved with unorthodox haste, driving down to Weybridge next morning, where Wallis eagerly explained it all again.

"It seems," Tizard said when he had finished, "that the main thing to establish is whether this freak of yours will really work, and if so how we go about putting it into practice."

At Teddington, he said, was a huge ship-testing tank which would be ideal for experiments. He also thought there should be more tests to check how much explosive would theoretically punch a hole in a dam.

"I think I know just the thing," said Wallis, whose "damology" researches had been fanatical. "There's a small disused dam in Radnorshire; no earthly use any more as a dam and won't ever be. We could try and knock it down."

"Who owns it?" Tizard asked.

"Birmingham Corporation." Wallis knew all the answers.

"We'll try them," Tizard said, and Birmingham Corporation, with a little prodding, said yes.

It was a nice little dam, about 150 feet long and quite thick, curving gracefully across the mouth of a reach of Rhayader Lake, high in the Welsh hills west of Leominster. The corporation had built a bigger dam across the mouth of the lake to feed a little river that tumbled out of the hills.

Wallis estimated that the old dam would have a fifth of the resistance of the Moehne, an ideal test model. He calculated the smallest charge that should knock it down and set off with a packet of RDX and some explosives engineers. Wrapped against the raw mountain wind, he wasted little time, measured out the charge, tamped it in a sealed casing and lowered it deep into the water against the dam wall. Behind the rocks, his mouth dry with anxiety, he pressed the plunger and the hills echoed with sound. Water spurted a hundred feet high, the lake whipped into fury, and as the water plunged back into the void, the concrete crumbled and a hissing flood burst into the main lake. Wallis, pink with glee, saw there was a ragged hole in the dam 15 feet across and about 12 feet deep.

For the next five months he experimented whenever he could in the tank at Teddington, an enormous thing well over a hundred feet long. He wanted to find out exactly how to control a skipping missile, so that after a given number of bounces over a given distance he could make it reach a certain given point at a certain minimum speed and height. At this ultimate spot the missile would have to be either slithering across the water or only just a fraction above it. He had to find out the best shape to use and the best combination of weight of missile, and height, speed and power of release. And what a headache it was, too. He had a spring-loaded catapult so that he could measure the force behind it, and began to accumulate an extraordinary number of combinations of heights, shapes, weights, speeds and distances. Hundreds and hundreds of times he shot his little missiles across the surface of the water and they skipped and skipped and skipped in little splashes, some of them foundering in mid-stream, some of them foundering three-quarters of the way along, some of them cracking against the end of the tank nearly fifty yards away at this height or that height, and one or two even bouncing over the end. And all this time Wallis was also trying to do his usual work at Vickers.

He filled notebook after notebook with his records and calculations and slowly, as he pored over them at nights assessing the results, certain conclusions began to emerge from all the figures and facts. For one thing some sort of regular shaped missile gave the most consistent results. Something, for instance, like a round ball, such as a golf ball, because every time it skipped and came down and hit the water again it was the same shaped surface that hit the water. That was the only thing that enabled one to predict a bounce. Any irregular shape would only give irregular bounces. He took to concentrating on firing golf balls and bit by bit found he could so adjust the height and strength of his catapult that he could make a ball slither neatly up to the far wall of the tank. There are ways of calculating from scale experiments how a full-sized object will perform. Or that is, how a full-sized object *should* perform if everything goes according to plan and nothing has been overlooked. By the middle of 1942 Wallis was satisfied he knew enough to make a 5-ton bomb skip under control for half a mile! It would look something like a big round ball of steel and he didn't quite know whether to call it a mine or a bomb.

Tizard was pleased, but Tizard was an adviser, not all-powerful; the task was to get executive officials keen. Wallis saw several officials, received tea and courtesy, even compliments, but not enough action to please him. Two high executives in particular who could have started things moving seemed irritatingly cautious.

Then one of the several government operational research

committees gave Wallis permission to build six half-size prototypes of his new bomb, purely for experiment, and told him he could convert a Wellington to drop them.

In a few weeks the casings were finished, big steel balls about four feet across. Wallis filled them with a harmless substitute the same weight as RDX, and at 3 p.m. on December 4, 1942, the converted Wellington took off from Weybridge with the first bomb on board and Mutt Summers in the pilot's seat, Wallis crouched in the nose as bomb-aimer, to test-drop off Chesil Beach on the south coast. They were not going to worry too much this time about precise speed and height. About fifty feet up and about 200 m.p.h. and, for the time being, never mind exactly how far the bomb went. It should, however, bounce cleanly about half-a-mile. Something near enough to that would do for the first test. The first thing was to see whether a few tons of steel ball *would* bounce according to theory.

Off Chesil Beach Summers dived low over the water, Wallis pressed the button and watched the big black bomb rattle clear of its stowage. It took so long it seemed like slow-motion, and then it hit and vanished in a sheet of hissing white spray. Staring tensely down out of the bomb-aimer's compartment Wallis watched with painful anxiety for it to appear. Just for a moment nothing seemed to happen and then out of the spray lurched the black ball looking somehow misshapen. It fell back into the water quite quickly, lurched drunkenly up again, hit once more, skipped another short distance and then slithered a few yards and vanished into the green depths. It didn't seem to have travelled more than about two hundred yards and Wallis looked down, puzzled, not quite knowing what to think. It had worked but not the way it was supposed to. Something was wrong. Summers turned the aeroplane back towards Weybridge and Wallis, on the way back, trying to imagine what could have gone wrong, remembered the misshapen look about the bomb. He decided that the casing had not been strong enough. It must have crushed a little under the impact, making the bounces unpredictable and sluggish. When they landed he ordered the cases of the remaining bombs to be strengthened.

On December 12 he and Summers took off with a strengthened bomb. Off Chesil Beach, Wallis watched the bomb going down, holding his breath, and feeling his mouth dry with anxiety. Again the hissing sheet of spray as it hit, and then: Oh the thrill, out of the spray the black ball came soaring a hundred yards across the water, hit with another flashing white feather of spray and soared out again, hit again, and again, the distances shortening every time until at last, after what looked like nearly half a mile, it slithered to a foaming stop and sank. Summers had banked the aeroplane round and they could both look down on that glorious sight of the long necklace of white foaming scars on the water where the bomb had hit. Wallis had seldom known such a moment of glad triumph. He crawled half-way out of the nose to look up and grin at Summers above in the cockpit. The engines were making too much noise to talk but Summers grinned down at him, gave him the thumbs-up sign and an enormous wink.

In the next three days he and Summers dropped three more bombs and they worked every time. They took a movie cameraman with them on these flights and got undeniable evidence that it worked.

On the strength of that Winterbotham arranged an interview for Wallis with the Ministry of Supply's scientific tribunal to assess new weapons. The tribunal watched his films and let it be known that the report would be favourable.

With his films Wallis made a new assault on the two cautious officials. They were still non-committal, but it seemed to Wallis a little less inflexibly so.

Slowly the weeks dragged by with no break-through, and Wallis was sinking into despair again when one day he got a call from one of the two cautious ones, giving him permission to go ahead with the preliminary design of a full-sized bomb. The official tempered his joy by telling him not to expect too much.

Further work would depend on whether it would dislocate work on a new bomber.

This was early February, 1943, and the best time to smash the dams was in May, when they were full. There was still just time. Wallis worked late over his plans and on the eighth day had them virtually finished when the bombshell dropped. One of the cautious ones 'phoned, ordering him to stop work on the big bomb. There was to be no further action on it.

Wallis went grimly next day to the big tank at Teddington, sank two glass air-tight tanks in the water, putting an arc-light in one and inducing a slight young woman to go into the other with a movie camera. She and the camera could just fit in. He fired a missile across the water, and as it slithered against the end of the tank and sank, the girl filmed its under-water progress. It was a beautiful film; clearly it showed the little sphere rolling down what would represent the dam wall deep under the water to the bottom of the tank.

Next he bailed up Summers and demanded an interview with Air Marshal Sir Arthur Harris, chief of Bomber Command. Summers had known Harris for years, well enough to call him by his first name, which few people dared to do. Harris, it was freely acknowledged, could crush a seaside landlady with a look.

Summers and Wallis drove into the wood outside High Wycombe where Harris had his headquarters, and as Wallis put his foot on the threshold of Harris's office the booming voice hit him like a shock wave.

"What is it you want? I've no time for you inventors. My boys' lives are too precious to be wasted by your crazy notions!"

It was enough to strike fear into the heart of the sturdiest inventor. Wallis almost baulked, then pressed on and there was the bulky figure of Harris, grey eyes staring coldly over the half-moon glasses perched on his nose.

"Well?" Harris was a man of few words and forceful ones.

"I have an idea for destroying German dams," Wallis said. "The effects on Germany would be enormous."

"I've heard about it. It's far-fetched."

Wallis said he'd like to explain it, and Harris gave a grunt which Wallis took for yes and went ahead, trying not to be too involved and yet show how he had proved the theory. At the end the bomber chief had absorbed it all. Not that there was any encouraging reaction. Harris said bluntly:

"If you think you're going to walk in and get a squadron of Lancasters out of me you've made a mistake. You're not!"

Wallis started to bristle and Summers, who knew Wallis's obstinacy and Harris's explosive temperament, kicked Wallis's shin under the desk. Wallis controlled himself.

"We don't want a squadron," he said, ". . . yet. We'd like a chance to prove it in trials with one Lancaster first."

Harris eyed him stonily. "Maybe," he said. "You *really* think you can knock a dam down with that thing."

"Yes," Wallis said. "Or it may take three or four. We can put them all in the same place."

Summers said peaceably, "We'll prove it'll work, Bert."

"Prove it and I'll arrange a squadron," Harris said, and then with his old fierceness, staring at Wallis, "but I'm tired of half-baked inventors trying to run things."

Summers kicked Wallis once more under the desk and broke the tension by saying, "We've got some films here that show clearly how it works."

"All right. Let's see them." They trooped out to the Command projection room, picking up Harris's chief lieutenant, Air Vice-Marshal Saundby, on the way. Harris curtly told the projectionist to clear out. "If it's as good as you say," he told Wallis, "there's no point letting everyone know. Saundby can run the films through."

Saundby's training had not concentrated much on film projection work and for a while there was a tangle of celluloid, but eventually he sorted it out, clicked the lights off and they watched in silence the antics of the bombs dropped at Chesil

34

Beach and the tricks of the model under the water at Teddington.

When the lights went up Harris had his poker face on. "Very interesting," he grunted. "I'll think it over."

Not long after, Wallis got a summons to a senior executive whom he knew quite well and who in the past had encouraged his bomb work.

"Wallis," he said, "I've been asked by——" (one of the two cautious ones) "to tell you to stop your nonsense about destroying dams. He tells me you're making a nuisance of yourself at the Ministry."

For a moment Wallis was stunned, then recovered and answered quietly, "If you think I'm not acting in the best interests of the war effort, I think I should offer to resign from all my work and try something else."

For the first and last time he saw the executive lose his temper. The man shot to his feet, smashed his fist on the desk and shouted "Mutiny!" Smashed his fist down again with another "Mutiny!" And again with a third explosive "Mutiny!" He subsided, red and quivering, and Wallis walked out of the room. He had lunch somewhere but does not remember where, and afterwards went and told the whole story to Sir Thomas Merton, one of the Supply Ministry's inventions tribunal. Merton promised support, but Wallis came away still depressed, knowing of nothing more he could do; it seemed too late now to organise things for the coming May, and after a couple of days he was resigned to it.

That was the day, February 26, he got a summons to the office of one of the cautious ones, and there he also found the senior executive who had shouted "Mutiny!" Proceedings opened by the cautious one saying, a little stiffly:

"Mr. Wallis, orders have been received that your dams project is to go ahead immediately with a view to an operation at all costs no later than May."

CHAPTER IV

A SQUADRON IS BORN

AFTER battling for so long, Wallis, in the weeks that followed, sometimes ruefully thought he had got more action than he could stand. Life was work from dawn till midnight, planning, draughting, thinking and discussing, grabbing a sandwich with one hand while the work went on.

He told his workers briefly what he wanted them to do, but not what the bombs were to do, or when, or where. Only he, Harris and a selected few others knew that, and apart from them a curtain of secrecy came down. Each craftsman worked on one part and knew nothing of the others. One of the first things Wallis himself had to do was to work out at exactly what speed and height the aeroplane should fly when they dropped the bombs, so that the bombs would reach the dam wall at the right height and speed.

The full-size bomb was to be a steel sphere seven feet in girth. Roy Chadwick, chief Avro designer, started taking the bomb doors off Lancasters and doing other strange things to them so they could carry it. Explosives experts, tactical authorities, secret service men and hundreds of others had a part in it, and over Germany every day a fast Mosquito flew 25,000 feet over the dams taking photographs. Deep in the underground vaults of Bomber Command men studied the photographs through thick magnifying glasses to check the level of the rising water and the defences. If the secret leaked out they would see the extra flak and the raid would have to be called off. It was going to be suicidal enough as it was. There seemed to be at least six gun positions around the Moehne alone, and that was no matter for comfort because the bombs would have to be dropped from very low level, so low that a pilot could lean out and almost dangle his fingers in the water. They would have to fly between two towers on top of the dam, and some of the guns were in these towers.

The Mosquitoes flew a devious way and crossed the dams as though by accident so the Germans would not be suspicious. An ugly sign appeared in the first few days: photographs showed the anti-torpedo boom in front of the Moehne was being repaired; it had been loose and untidy, and now it was being tightened. Nothing else appeared to be happening though, and after a while it was reasonable to assume that it was only a periodical check. While the work pressed on in England, it seemed that the Germans were doing nothing significant.

At his headquarters in the wood Air Marshal Arthur Harris ("Bert" to his friends and "Bomber" to the public) had been pondering how the attack should be made—and who should make it. On March 15 he sent for Air Vice-Marshal the Honourable Ralph Cochrane, who two days before had become Air Officer Commanding No. 5 (Bomber) Group.

"I've got a job for you, Cocky," Harris said and told him about Wallis's weird bomb and what he proposed to do with it. At the end he said: "I know it sounds far-fetched, but I think it has a good chance."

Cochrane said: "Well, sir, I've known Wallis for twenty-five years. He's a wonderful engineer and I've never known him not to produce what he says he will."

"I hope he does it again now," Harris said. "You know how he works. I want you to organise the raid. Ask for anything you want, as long as it's reasonable."

Cochrane thought for a moment.

"It's going to need some good aircrews," he said. "I think I'd better screen one of my squadrons right away and start them on intensive training."

"I don't want to do that," Harris said. "I don't want to take a single squadron out of the line if I can help it, or interfere with any of the main force. What I have in mind is a new squadron, say, of experienced people who're just finishing a tour. Some of the keen chaps won't mind doing another trip. Can you find enough in your group?"

"Yes, sir." Cochrane asked Harris if he wanted anyone in particular to command the new squadron, and Harris said:

"Yes, Gibson."

Cochrane nodded in satisfaction, and ten minutes later, deep in thought, he was driving back to the old Victorian mansion outside Grantham that was 5 Group Headquarters. There could probably have been no better choice than Cochrane for planning the raid. A spare man with a lean face, his manner was crisp and decisive, perfectly reflecting his mind. The third son of a noble Scottish family, he was climbing to the top on his own ability; he had perhaps the most incisive brain in the R.A.F. His god was efficiency and he sought it uncompromisingly—almost ruthlessly according to some of his men, who were afraid of him, but his aircrews would do anything he asked, knowing that it would be meticulously planned.

Moreover, Cochrane knew Wallis well; had worked with him in the Royal Naval Air Service in World War I, flying his experimental airships and testing the world's first airship mooring mast, which Wallis had designed. Ever since then Cochrane had had a quick sympathy for the scientific approach.

That night a nuggetty little man with a square, handsome face, named Guy Gibson, took off on the last trip of his third tour. If he got back he was due for leave and a rest, having been on ops almost constantly since the war started. The target was Stuttgart and his Lancaster was laden with one of the new 8,000-lb. "blockbusters" (not the penetrating "earthquake" type that Wallis envisaged, but bombs had made startling strides in the past year).

An engine failed on the way to Stuttgart and the aircraft would not hold her height. Gibson eased her out of the stream, dropping towards the ground, but headed on. The last trip of a tour is an ordeal with its hopes of a six-months' reprieve. Before take-off the reprieve seems so near and yet so far, and waiting to get it over is not pleasant. Gibson took a chance rather than turn back and go through the waiting again.

Over Stuttgart he had the other three engines shaking the aircraft at full power and managed to drag up to a safe enough height to drop his bomb, then dived to the dark anonymity of earth and hugged the ground all the way back. That was Gibson's 173rd trip. He was a wing commander with the D.S.O. and D.F.C. Aged twenty-five.

He woke late, head still ringing with the engine noise, and lay curled up, half thinking, half dreaming of leave in Cornwall. That morning his leave was cancelled and, to his dismay, he was posted to 5 Group Headquarters.

A day or so later he was shown into Cochrane's office and saluted smartly.

"Ah, Gibson," Cochrane said. "Firstly, my congratulations on the bar to your D.S.O."

"Thank you, sir."

"Would you like to do one more trip?"

Gibson gulped and said, a little warily:

"What kind of trip, sir?"

"An important one. I can't tell you any more about it now except that you would command the operation."

Gibson said slowly, "Yes, I—I think so, sir," thinking of the flak and the fighters he hoped he had finished with for a time.

"Good; that's fine. I'll let you know more as soon as I can," and a moment later Gibson was outside the door, wondering what it was all about. He waited two days before Cochrane sent for him again, and this time another man was with him, Group Captain Charles Whitworth, who commanded the bomber base at Scampton, a stocky, curly-haired man of about thirty, with a long list of operations behind him and a D.S.O. and D.F.C. on his tunic. Gibson knew him and liked him.

Cochrane was friendly. "Sit down," he said and held out a cigarette. "I asked you the other day if you'd care to do another raid and you said you would, but I want to warn you that this will be no ordinary sortie and it can't be done for at least two months."

Gibson thought: "It's the *Tirpitz*. Why did I say yes!" The 45,000-ton "unsinkable" battleship was lying in a Norwegian fiord, a permanent menace to the Russia convoys and a lethal target to tackle.

Cochrane was still talking. "Training for this raid is so important that the Commander-in-Chief wants a special squadron formed. I want you to form it. You'd better use Whitworth's main base at Scampton. As far as aircrews are concerned, you'll want good ones; you'd better pick them yourself. I'm telling all the squadrons they'll have to give up some of their best crews. I'm afraid they won't like it, so try and take men who are near the end of their tours. There's a lot of urgency in this because you haven't got very long and training is going to be very important. Go to it as fast as you can and try and get your aircraft flying in four days."

"Well, er . . . what sort of training, sir?" Gibson asked. "And . . . what sort of target?"

"Low flying," Cochrane said. "You've got to be able to low-fly at night till it's second nature. No, I can't tell you the target yet. That's secret, but you've all got to be perfect at low flying. At night. It's going to be the only way, and I think you can do it. You're going to a place where it'd be wrong to send a single squadron at the normal height by itself."

Gibson knew what that meant. Germany! A single squadron at 15,000 feet would get all the night fighters. It was not so bad for the main force, the stream of hundreds of bombers; they confused the enemy radar, dispersed the fighters, and there was protection in numbers. Not so with a lone squadron. But low level, "on the deck," yes. Well, maybe! Well, it was going to be low level anyway. Over Germany! He knew a man named Martin who knew all about low flying over Germany. Gibson had met him when Martin was being decorated for it.

Outside the door Whitworth said, "See you at Scampton in a couple of days. I'll get things fixed up for you. I imagine you'll be having about seven hundred men."

Somewhat bewildered, Gibson went off to the S.O.A. to see how one went about forming a new squadron. A staff officer helped him pick aircrew from the group lists. Gibson knew most of the pilots—he got the staff man to promise him Martin and help him pick the navigators, engineers, bomb aimers, wireless operators and gunners; when they had finished they had 147 names—twenty-one complete crews, seven to a crew. Gibson had his own crew; they were just finishing their tour too, but they all wanted to come with him.

The Staff Officer Personnel told him how many men of different trades he wanted for his ground crews and promised to siphon off picked men from other squadrons and post them to Scampton in forty-eight hours.

The equipment officer promised to deliver ten Lancasters to Scampton within two days. Just for a start. More would follow. With them would come the spare spark plugs and tools, starter motors and drip trays, bomb dollies and winches, dope and paint and chocks and thermos flasks. Gibson was startled by the unending list. Another man promised the thousand and one items for the men: blankets and lorries and bootlaces, beer and socks, toilet paper and so on. He was two days on these details, helped by Cochrane's deputy, the S.A.S.O., Group Captain Harry Satterly, a big, smooth-faced man who was excellent at detail; and then it was all done—except for one thing.

"What squadron are you?" Satterly asked.

"What d'you mean, sir?"

"What number? You've got to have a number."

"Oh," said Gibson, "where d'you get that?"

"Somewhere in Air Ministry," Satterly said, "but they probably don't work so fast there. I'll get on to them and fix it up. Meantime you'd better call yourselves 'X Squadron'."

*   *   *

Just before dinner on March 21, Wing Commander Guy Gibson, D.S.O., D.F.C., commander of "X", the paper squadron, arrived at Scampton to take formal command. In the officers' mess he found some of his crews already arrived and the mess waiters looking curiously at them as they stood around with pints of beer in their fists. It was obvious they were not to be an ordinary squadron; the average age was about twenty-two but they were clearly veterans. D.F.C. ribbons were everywhere; they had all done one tour, and some had done two. Gibson moved among them, followed by the faithful Nigger, his black Labrador dog, who rarely left his heels.

From his old 106 Squadron, Gibson had brought three crews as well as his own—those of Hopgood, Shannon and Burpee. Hopgood was English, fair and good looking except for a long front tooth that stuck out at an angle. Dave Shannon, D.F.C., was a baby-faced twenty-year-old from Australia, but did not look any more than sixteen, so he was growing a large moustache to look older.

Gibson spotted Micky Martin with satisfaction. They had met at Buckingham Palace when Gibson was getting his D.S.O. and the King was pinning on the first of Martin's D.F.Cs. Though he came from Sydney, Martin was in the R.A.F., slight but good looking, with a wild glint in his eyes and a monstrous moustache that ended raggedly out by his ears. At the Palace they had talked shop and Martin had explained his low-flying system.

He had worked it out that if you flew lower than most bombers you would avoid the fighters; lower still and the heavy flak would all burst well above. And if you got right down to tree-top height you would be gone before the light flak could draw a bead on you. There was still the risk of balloons, but Martin reasoned there would not be any balloons along main roads or railways, so he followed those. He had had the same two gunners for two years. Toby Foxlee and Tammy Simpson both fellow-Australians, and on their low-level junkets they had become expert at picking off searchlights. Simpson and Foxlee had both come with him; he'd also brought an experienced navigator, a lean, long-chinned Australian called Jack Leggo, and his bomb aimer, Bob Hay, also Australian, had been a bombing expert at Group. Leggo was to be navigation officer of the new squadron, and Hay was to be bombing leader. It is unlikely that there was a finer crew in Bomber Command; hence Gibson's pleasure.

He had chosen "Dinghy" Young as his senior flight commander. Young had already ditched twice in his two tours, and both times got back home in his rubber dinghy. Bred in California, educated at Cambridge, he was a large, calm man whose favourite trick was to swallow a pint of beer without drawing breath.

Les Munro was a New Zealander, tall, blue-chinned and solemn, a little older than the others. He was standing by the bar looking into space when Gibson located him. "Glad to see you, Les," Gibson said. "I see you're setting a good example already, drinking a little and thinking a lot." Munro upended his pint and drained it. "No, sir," he said, "thinking a little and drinking a lot."

The other flight commander was Henry Maudslay, ex-50 Squadron, ex-Eton, an athlete, polished and quiet, not a heavy drinker. Towering above the rest was the blond head of a man who weighed nearly 15 stone, with a pink face and pale blue eyes; good looking in a rugged way. Joe McCarthy, from Brooklyn, U.S.A., former life-guard at Coney Island, had joined the R.A.F. before America came into the war.

No one knew what they were there for but, looking at the men around them, realised something special was in the wind. Someone finally asked Gibson what "the form" was and Gibson simply said: "I know less than you, old boy, but I'll see you all in the morning to give you what gen I can."

In the morning Gibson called all the crews to the long briefing room on top of station headquarters and said:

"I know you're wondering why you're here. Well, you're here as a crack squadron to do a special job which I'm told will have startling results and may shorten the war. I can't tell you what the target is or where it is. All I can tell you is you'll have to practise low flying day and night until you can do it with your eyes shut. . . ."

He went on to talk about training and organisation, and when it was over the crews trooped out with little flutters in their stomachs, the sort of feeling you get before a raid. It goes once you get into the air.

Dinghy Young and Maudslay were busy dividing the crews into flights and Gibson walked over to No. 2 hangar, the great steel shed that was to be squadron headquarters. Inside, a dapper little man with a toothbrush moustache broke off his interviewing and saluted smartly; Flight Sergeant "Chiefy" Powell had just arrived to be the squadron's disciplinary N.C.O. The ground crews were arriving in scores and Powell already had half of them organised in their billets and sections.

Cochrane rang Gibson: "I'm sending you over a list of lakes in England and Wales that I want photographed. Get someone on to it as soon as you can."

Gibson, who had learned not to ask questions, said, "Yes, sir," wondering when the fog of secrecy was going to lift.

Gibson spent hours interviewing his aircrews, sizing up the ones he didn't know, and found that some of the squadron commanders, told to send their best men, had played the age-old service game and got rid of a couple they did not want. Gibson told them to pack and go back. He walked into the mess bar just before dinner, tired but feeling they were getting somewhere, and Charles Whitworth buttonholed him.

"Well, Gibby," he said, "you're going to command 617 Squadron now."

The little man looked thunderstruck. "What!" he exploded. "617? I thought . . . I . . . Who and where are they?"

"Here," said Whitworth peaceably. "You. Your new number. Someone in Air House has moved off his bottom. Your Squadron marking letters are AJ."

He called for a pint each and they drank to 617 Squadron.

CHAPTER V

OVER THE HURDLES

HUMPHRIES, the new adjutant, arrived next afternoon; a little fair-haired man, only twenty-eight, he was keen on flying but his eyes had stopped him. Gibson told Humphries as much as he knew himself, and as Humphries was leaving his office Gibson said:

"I don't know yet what it's all about, but I gather this squadron will either make history or be wiped out."

In the morning the curtain lifted a little. Gibson got a call from Satterly, who told him to catch a certain train to Weybridge, where he would be met at the station.

"May I know who I'm meeting, sir?"

"He'll know you," Satterly said.

Gibson walked out of Weybridge Station at half-past two and a big man squeezed behind the wheel of a tiny Fiat said, "Hello, Guy!"

"Mutt," Gibson said, surprised. "Are you the man I'm looking for?"

"If you're the man I'm waiting for, I am," Summers said. "Jump in." They drove down the winding tree-lined road that leads to Vickers and went past the main gates without turning in. "What's this all about, Mutt?" Gibson said, unable to hold back any longer.

"You'll find out." He turned off up a side road to the left. "You wanted to be a test pilot for me once. D'you remember?"

"I remember." That was when he had first met Summers. It must have been eight years ago now, back in 1935, when he was eighteen. He had wanted to fly, so he had got an introduction to Summers at Vickers and asked about becoming a

Vickers test pilot. "Go and join the Air Force and learn to fly first." Summers had advised.

"You'll be doing some testing soon," Summers said. "Not for me exactly, but quite a test." He turned in some double gates and they pulled up outside the house at Burhill. Summers led the way into a room with windows looking over the golf course, and a white-haired man got up from a desk.

"I'm glad you've come," Wallis said. "Now we can get down to it. There isn't a great deal of time left. I don't suppose you know much about the weapon?"

"Weapon?" Gibson said. "I don't know anything about anything."

Wallis blinked. "Don't you even know the target?"

"Not the faintest idea."

"My dear boy," Wallis said in a sighing and faintly horrified voice. "My dear boy." He wandered over to the window and looked out, pondering. "That makes it very awkward. This is dreadfully secret and I can't tell anyone whose name isn't on this list." He waved a bit of paper in Gibson's direction and Gibson could see there were only about half a dozen names on it.

Summers said, "This is silly."

"I know," Wallis said gloomily. "Well, my dear boy . . . I'll tell you as much as I dare and hope the A.O.C. will tell you the rest when you get back." Gibson waited curiously, and finally Wallis went on: "There are certain objects in enemy territory which are very big and quite vital to his war effort. They're so big that ordinary bombs won't hurt them, but I got an idea for a special type of big bomb."

He told Gibson about the shock waves and his weird idea for dropping bombs exactly in the right spot. Gibson was looking baffled trying to follow the shock wave theory.

"You've seen it working in pubs, Guy," Summers said. "A dozen times. The shove-ha'penny board. Remember how you get two or three discs lying touching and flick another one in behind them. The shock waves go right through them but

46

they all stay where they are except the front one, and that goes skidding off. That's the shock wave."

"Come and I'll show you," Wallis said and led Gibson into a tiny projection room. Wallis thumbed the switches and a flickering screen lit up with the title "Most Secret Trial No. 1." A Wellington dived into view over water and what looked like a big black ball fell from it, seemed to drop slowly and then was hidden in spray as it hit. Gibson started in amazement as out of the spray the black ball shot, bounced a hundred yards, bounced again in a cloud of spray and went on bouncing for what seemed an incredibly long time before it vanished. He was still staring at the screen when the lights went up again.

"Well, that's my secret bomb," Wallis said. "That's how we . . . how *you're* going to put it in the right place."

"Over water?" Gibson said, fishing for a clue.

"Yes," but Wallis avoided the subject of the target. "Over water at night or in the early morning when it's very flat, and maybe there will be fog. Now, can you fly to the limits I want, a speed of two hundred and forty miles per hour, at sixty feet over smooth water, and be able to bomb accurately?"

"It's terribly hard to judge your height over water," Gibson said, "particularly smooth water. How much margin of error is allowed?"

"None. That's the catch. Sixty feet. Just that. No more. No less. So the aiming will be accurate."

"Well . . . we can try. I suppose we can find a way."

"There's so *much* to do." Wallis sighed.

On the way back to Scampton, Gibson puzzled over the target. The only likely ones, he decided, were either the *Tirpitz* or the U-boat pens, and he shuddered a little at the thought of a low-level attack on them. They would be smothered in guns. At Scampton he found some Lancasters had arrived and ground crews were checking them over. In the morning he told his senior men what height they would have to bomb at but nothing about the bomb itself.

Dinghy Young said: "We'll have to do all the training we can by moonlight, and you don't get much reliable moonlight in this country."

"Could we fly around with dark glasses on?" Maudslay asked.

"No, that's no good. You can't see your instruments properly."

Gibson said he'd heard of a new type of synthetic night training. They put transparent amber screens round the perspex and the pilot wore blue glasses; it was like looking out on moonlight but you could still see your instruments. He would see if Satterly could get them some.

Leggo was worried about navigation. Low-flying navigation is different. You don't see much of the area when you're low, so they were going to need large-scale maps with plenty of detail. Large-scale maps meant constant changing and awkward unfolding. He suggested they use strip maps wound on rollers; navigators could prepare their own. And if they were flying low, radio was not going to be much use for navigation. It would be mostly map reading.

Bill Astell, deputy A Flight commander, took off the first Lancaster and was away five hours, coming back with photographs of lakes all over the north country. Gibson laid out ten separate routes for the crews to practise over, and in the days that followed the Lancasters were nosing thunderously into the air all day and cruising at 100 feet over the flat fens of Lincolnshire, Suffolk and Norfolk.

Flying low seems faster and is more exciting, also more dangerous. There is the temptation to slip between chimneys or lift a wingtip just over a tree, and the R.A.F. was losing a lot of aircraft every month from fatal low-flying accidents. It was (naturally) strictly forbidden, and the pilots were delighted to be ordered to do it. Across several counties outraged service police reached for notebooks and took the big AJ aircraft letters as they roared over their heads; the complaints came flooding into Gibson's office, and with smug rectitude he tore them up.

After a few days they came down to 50 feet and flew longer

routes, stretching out to the north country, threading through the valleys of the Pennines, climbing and diving over the Welsh mountains, then down to Cornwall and up to Scotland, eventually as far as the Hebrides, winging low over the white horses while the pilots flew steady courses and the rest of the crews gave a hand with the map reading.

Gibson took his own Lancaster, G for George, and flew over a lake in the Pennines, to test the business of flying accurately at 60 feet over water. Diving over the hills he flattened out over the lake, then pulled up over the hills at the far end; tried it several times and found it fairly easy to keep his altimeter needle steady around 60 feet. But the trial meant little. Over Germany barometric pressures would be unpredictable, and altimeters work off barometric pressure. He had to find some way of judging his height without relying much on the altimeter. Practice might do it.

He tried again at dusk with fog drifting over the lake, and it was different. Not pleasantly. The smooth water merged with the gloom and he found he did not have much idea about judging height. They very nearly went into the lake and as he pulled sharply up there was a grunt over the intercom as Trevor-Roper in the rear turret saw the ripples on the water from their slipstream. Even Spam Spafford, Gibson's chunky bomb aimer, was shaken. He had had a disconcerting vision of the looming water from the nose perspex.

Gibson flew back and told Cochrane that if he could not find some way of judging height accurately there would be no chance of doing the raid.

"There's still time to worry about that," Cochrane said. "Just now I want you to have a look at models of your targets." He waved a hand at three packing cases in a corner of his office and Gibson eyed them curiously. "You can't train your men properly unless you know what they are, so I'm letting you know now, but you'll be the only man in the squadron to know. Keep it that way."

A corporal brought in a hammer, and Cochrane sent him out

D   49

of the room while Gibson gently prised the lids loose and lifted the battens. He stood looking down at the models, and his first reaction was a feeling of tremendous relief. Thank God, it wasn't the *Tirpitz*! It took him a couple of seconds after that to realise they were dams. One was the Moehne, and the other two the Eder and the Sorpe, handsome models that showed not only the dams but the countryside in detail for miles around, as though photographs had taken on a third dimension. There were the flat surfaces of the lakes, the hills, winding rivers and the mosaic of fields and hedges. And in the middle the dams. Gibson stood looking for a long time and then Cochrane laid the lids back over them.

"Now you've seen what you've got to attack," he said. "Go and see Wallis again and come and see me when you get back."

The first thing Wallis said, eagerly, was:

"How did you get on?"

"All right by day," Gibson said, "but not so good at night. In fact, flying level at night over water at sixty feet seems pretty nearly impossible."

"We'll work out some way of doing it. Now I'll tell you more about this Downwood business."

"Downwood?"

"The code name for the raid." Wallis explained how the bombs were to explode deep against the dam walls.

"I've calculated that the first one ought at least to crack them, and then more bombs in the same place should shift the cracked wall back till it topples over . . . helped, of course, by the water pressure. The best times, of course, are when the dams are full. That will be in May. You'll need moonlight, and there's a full moon from the thirteenth to the nineteenth of May."

"Only about six weeks."

"Yes."

"Oh," Gibson said and went back thoughtfully to Scampton.

The synthetic night-flying gear arrived, transparent amber screens and blue glasses; "two-stage amber," it was called.

The screens were fitted in the cockpits, pilots donned their glasses and flying by day was exactly like flying in moonlight. they flew thousands of miles with them, first at 150 feet and then, as Gibson decided they were good enough, at 50 feet, the bomb aimers looking through the nose to warn of trees and hills.

Gibson took the screens and blue lenses away and sent the crews on low-level night cross-countries, first aircraft singly, and then, when the moon was right, in loose formations. Two crews were too keen and came back with branches and leaves in their radiators.

Gibson was on the move from dawn to midnight every day, usually careering about on a little auto-bike from flights to armoury, to orderly room and so on. When he flew he kept his auto-bike in the hangar, apparently against some fiddling regulation because Scampton's zealous service policeman told Chiefy Powell the auto-bike would have to be moved.

Powell eyed him flintily. "You'd better see the owner," he said. "I don't think he'll move it."

"I'll see him all right," said the sergeant, "and he'll move it too."

So Chiefy took him in to see Gibson and shut the door behind him. There was a violent roaring behind the door and a white-faced sergeant came out.

The bike stayed where it was.

The crews practised low-level bombing on the range at Wainfleet, diving over the sand dropping 11½-lb. practice bombs with the low-level bombsight. The drops were not nearly accurate enough and Bob Hay said so disgustedly. Gibson took the problem to Cochrane.

Two days later a Wing Commander Dann, from the Ministry of Aircraft Production, called on Gibson.

"I hear you're having bombsight trouble for the dams raid."

"How do you know about this?" Gibson said.

"I've been let into it because I'm supposed to be a sighting expert," Dann explained. "I think I can solve your troubles. You may have noticed there are a couple of towers on top of each dam wall. We've measured them from the air and they're six hundred feet apart. Now this"—and he produced some drawings of a very elementary gadget—"is how we do it."

It was laughably simple; a carpenter ran up one of the gadgets in five minutes out of bits of spare wood. The base was a small triangle of plywood with a peephole at one angle and two nails stuck in the other corners. "You look through the peephole," Dann said, "and when the two towers on the dams are in line with the nails, you press the button. You'll find it'll drop in the right spot but you'll have to stick right on the speed."

Gibson shook his head in wonder. Workmen put two dummy towers on the dam across the neck of a midland lake, the bomb aimers knocked up their own sights and on his first try one of them dropped eight practice bombs with an average error of only 4 yards.

Still the problem of the height. Gibson tried repeatedly to see if practice made perfect, but it didn't. After his fifth try Dinghy Young landed and said, "It's no use. I can't see how we're going to do it. Why can't we use radio altimeters?"

Gibson said he had thought of them a long time ago but they were not sensitive enough.

Time was getting short. Gibson got a call from Satterly. "They've finished the first two prototypes of the new bomb," Satterly said. "Fly down to Herne Bay tomorrow and watch the test drops. Take your bombing leader with you." That was April 15.

Wallis met them and next morning they drove out to a bare beach near Reculver. Half a mile back from the sea M.I.5 had cordoned the area off.

"I'm sorry to get you up so early," said the ever-courteous Wallis, "but the tide is up and that is the right time. We want to walk out at low tide and see how the bomb stands up to the shock of dropping."

In the east came two specks which grew into Lancasters, heading low over the shallows towards two white buoys bobbing on the water. "The other one's the camera aircraft," Wallis said as they watched them, and as the noise of engines filled the air Wallis was shouting above the roar, "He's high. He's too high." He sounded agitated. They swept up side by side and a great black thing dropped slowly away under the nearer one. It hit and vanished in a sheet of spray that hissed up towards the plane. For a moment there was nothing but the spray, and then out of it the fragments came flying.

"Broken," Wallis said and stood there very still. He took a deep breath. "They said it wouldn't work. Too big and heavy and the case too light. We've got another in the hangars. We'll try it this afternoon. The aircraft was too high."

Men worked hard that afternoon to strengthen the case of the second bomb while Wallis stripped to his underpants and waded to his neck in the freezing water, feeling with his feet for the fragments of the broken one. A launch took the broken bits on board and Wallis climbed in shivering, oblivious of everything but the ragged edges where the metal had burst.

They were on the dunes again as the sun was going down and the two aircraft came in sight, lower this time. Mutt Summers in the bomb plane was holding her steady at 50 feet. The suspense was painful. The black monster dropped away below, and again the water gushed skywards as it hit and out of the foaming cloud came the flying fragments as it broke.

Wallis said "Oh, my God!" And then out of the spray the jagged bulk of the main body of the bomb lurched into the air and skipped erratically for a hundred yards or so before it rolled under the water. Wallis stared in silence for a few seconds with the look of a man who has lost a shilling and found threepence. He sighed, and said, "Well, it's a bit better than this morning."

(In the Lancaster, Summers was not happy. A lump of the casing had hit the elevators and one of them had jammed. The plane could just hold its height while Summers was holding his breath. He did a wide gentle turn and made a heart-stopping landing on the long runway at Manston with the trimmers.)

Wallis told Gibson: "We've still got a lot of work to do on the bomb; but don't worry, it's going to be all right." Gibson and Hay took off in a little plane for Scampton and a few hundred feet up the engine coughed and died. There was only one way to go and that was down, but all the good fields were still covered with poles so the Germans could not land troops in an invasion. Gibson did his best to steer between them but a wingtip hit a pole, and as the aircraft slewed the other wing hit and they finished up sitting in a ball of crumpled duralumin, but were able to climb out.

A man came haring across the field, and when he saw they were not badly hurt he said severely, "I think they teach you young fellows to fly too early"; and then a policeman arrived and said unemotionally, "I'm glad to see our landing devices work."

Gibson and Hay went back to Scampton by train, and on the way Gibson thought up a scheme to overcome the height problem: to dangle a long wire under the aircraft with a weight on it so it would skim the water when the aircraft was exactly at 60 feet. Full of hope, he tried it in G for George, but it didn't work. At speed the line trailed out almost straight behind.

Cochrane set the "back-room boys" to work on the problem and a day later Ben Lockspeiser, of the Ministry of Aircraft Production, arrived at Grantham with an idea. It was absurd to think how simple it was—and how effective. "Put a spotlight under the nose," he said, "and another one under the belly, both pointing down and inwards so they converge at sixty feet. When the two spots come together on the water, there you are!"

Maudslay flew a Lancaster down to Farnborough and they fitted two spotlights on it the same day. Coming back he made test runs across the aerodrome and it worked beautifully. Maudslay said it was easy to get the circles of light together and keep them there. The idea was that they should touch each other, forming a figure "8." He had Urquhart, his navigator, leaning his head out of the perspex observation blister behind the pilot, looking down at the ground and saying, "Down,

down, down . . . up a bit . . . O.K.," and that was the procedure
they adopted. They all tried it over Derwent Water using the
same drill, and could fly to within 2 feet with wonderful con-
sistency. Everyone was pleased but not exactly in ecstasy,
because the same thought was in all their minds. An aircraft
pelting up to a defended target at 60 feet did not make the crew
very good insurance risks. And when it was showing lights
too . . .

Down at Weybridge Wallis was still trying to strengthen the
bomb and things were not going well. On April 22 they flew
the first new model over to Reculver and dropped it; it didn't
break up, but the case crushed on impact once more and, after
two erratic hops, the bomb went straight to the bottom. The
tormented Wallis had a pretty problem now. There was no
time to re-design the casing. Three weeks to the date for the
raid and if they couldn't make the time it would have to be
put off for another year; probably, in view of official scepticism,
for ever. The water in the dams was rising. In the next week
Wallis got little sleep while he spent long hours working to find
little ways of making the casing just that much stronger. He
was living on hope.

On April 29 they finished another modified bomb and Vickers
test pilot Shorty Longbottom flew it to Reculver for the drop.
It was pouring with rain and Wallis, out on the dunes, did not
even notice it as he eyed the Lancaster diving out of the east
towards the markers. Longbottom had her tucked down neatly
to 60 feet at 258 indicated air speed, squinting through the rain
squalls to hold his height and see the markers. The bomb fell
slowly, and then out of the usual shower of spray it came
bounding in majestic and perfect flight—and went on bouncing
for half-a-mile. Down on the dunes, Longbottom, banking
round, saw a white dot bobbing about. Wallis had taken his
hat off and was waving it in the air, dancing and shouting while
the rain ran down his face.

CHAPTER VI

TAKE-OFF

EARLY in May a strange-looking aircraft flew over Scampton, the first of the modified Lancasters. It looked like a designer's nightmare; the bomb doors were gone and the mid-upper turret and some of the armour, and there was a lot of queer junk sticking out underneath. It looked better for walking than flying. The rest of the modified aircraft arrived in the next few days. The pilots found they flew all right, though they had lost a little performance.

A couple of days later, on May 8, Gibson, Martin and Hopgood flew three of them down to Manston, and Martin and Hopgood watched goggle-eyed while a bomb was loaded into each. Two dummy towers had been put up on the water at Reculver, and the three aircraft had a run at them, dropping the bombs with the quaint plywood bombsights. It was beautiful to watch. Three enchanting direct hits. Three times in a row the great spheres skipped between the dummy towers along the surface of the water.

The worry and rush were telling on Gibson now; he was irritable and a carbuncle was forming painfully on his face so that he could not get his oxygen mask on. Not that he was going to need oxygen on a low-level raid, but his microphone was in the mask. He went to the doctor, and in his detached professional way the doctor said, "This means you're overworked. I'm afraid you'll have to take a couple of weeks off"; and Gibson stared at him ludicrously and laughed in his face.

He planned to control the raid by plain-language radio, and Cochrane got them VHF fighter sets. Hutchison, squadron signals leader, set them up first in the crew room so they could have dummy practices on R/T procedure.

The stage was nearly set, but at Bomber Command and at Grantham there was secret dismay. For three days the Mosquito had been bringing back photographs that showed mysterious activity on top of the Moehne Dam. The dark shapes of some new structures had been appearing, growing from day to day. There were about five sets of them, visible as short black rectangles. The interpretive experts puzzled over them for hours, blowing up the photos as large as the grain would take, examining them under strong light and through magnifying glasses nearly as strong as microscopes. The structures threw shadows across the dam top, and they measured the shadows but still were baffled. There seemed to be only one answer—new gun positions. There must have been a security leak somewhere.

At midnight on May 13 a convoy of covered lorries rolled round the perimeter track to the bomb dump at Scampton; a cordon of guards gathered round and the bombs were trollied into the dump and hidden under tarpaulins. They had only just been filled and were still warm to the touch.

Gibson drove off to see Satterly and plan the routes for the raid, taking with him Group Captain Pickard (of "F for Freddy") because he was a "gen" man on German flak positions, and on a low-level raid there is nothing more important than plotting a track between the known flak. They spread their maps out on the floor and carefully pencilled in two separate tracks that wound in and out of the red blotches of the known flak. They plotted two more widely differing routes for the trip home so that any flak aroused on the way in would watch out in vain for the return.

The attack would be in three waves, Gibson leading nine aircraft on the southern route, Munro leading others on the northern, and five aircraft taking off a couple of hours later to act as a reserve. If the Moehne, Eder and Sorpe were not smashed by the first two waves, Gibson would call up the reserves. If they *were* smashed the reserves would bomb three smaller dams in the same area, the Schwelm, Ennerpe and Dieml.

Accurate navigation was going to be vital or there were going to be sudden deaths. The pencilled tracks had to go perilously near some of the red flak areas.

"Doc" Watson and his armourers were loading the bombs into the Lancasters. Martin watched Watson winching the bomb up into his aircraft, "P for Peter" (or, as Martin always insisted, "P for Popsie"). "Just exactly how *do* these bombs work, Doc?" he asked.

"I know as much as you do, Micky," Watson said busily. "Nothing!"

"Ar, what do they pay you for?" Half an hour later the bomb was in position and he and Bob Hay, Leggo, Foxlee, Simpson and Whittaker were crawling about inside the aircraft seeing that everything was in order when a fault developed in the bomb release circuit, the release snapped back and there was a crunch as the giant black thing fell and crashed through the concrete hardstanding, embedding itself 4 inches into the earth below. Relieved of the weight, "P for Popsie" kicked a little from the expanding oleo legs of the under-carriage.

Martin said, "What's that?" There was a startled yell from an armourer outside and Martin yelled, "Hey, the thing's fallen off!"

"Release wiring must be faulty," Hay said professionally, and then it dawned on him and he said in a shocked voice, "It might have fused itself." He ran, yelling madly, out of the nose. "Get out of here. She'll go off in less than a minute." Bodies came tumbling out of the escape hatches, saw the tails of the armourers vanishing in the distance and set off after them. Martin jumped into the flight van near by and, with a grinding of gears, roared off to get Doc Watson. He had his foot hard down on the accelerator and swears that a terrified armourer passed him on a push-bike. He ran into Watson's office and panted out the news and Watson said philosophically, "Well, if she was going off she'd have gone off by this."

He got into the flight van and drove over to the deserted plane. Pale faces peeped out, watching him from deep shelters round the perimeter track hundreds of yards away, and Watson turned and bellowed, "O.K. Flap's over. It's not fused."

The squadron was fused though; painfully aware that something tremendous was about to happen. The aircraft were there, the bombs were there, both had been put together and crews were trained to the last gasp. Now was the time, Gibson knew, nerves would be tautening as they wondered whether there was going to be a reasonable chance of coming back or whether they would be dead in forty-eight hours. (And it was not only the aircrews who were tensed. Anne Fowler was too; she was a dark slim W.A.A.F. officer at Scampton, and in the past few weeks she and the boyish David Shannon had become a most noticeable twosome.)

Perhaps the least affected was the wiry and rambunctious Martin. Aged twenty-four, he had already decided that he was going to die, if not on this raid then on some other. Before the war was over anyway. During his first few "ops" he had often had sleepless nights or dreamed of burning aircraft. He saw all his friends on his squadron get "the chop" one after the other till they were all gone and knew it would only be a question of time before he would probably join them. So finally he had accepted the fact that in a fairly short time, barring miracles, he was going to die, not pleasantly. That was his strength and largely why he was so boisterous. Having accepted that, the next step was automatic: to fill every day with as many of the fruits of life as possible. He did so with vigour.

It was a corollary, more than a paradox, that he was not suicidal in the air but audacious in a calculating way, measuring every risk and if it were worth while, taking it, spinning it out as long as he could, but making every bomb tell. He did not believe in miracles.

* * *

59

On the morning of May 15, you could clearly sense the tension, more so when word spread that the A.O.C. had arrived. Cochrane saw Gibson and Whitworth alone and was brief and businesslike.

"If the weather's right you go tomorrow night. Start briefing your crews this afternoon and see that your security is foolproof."

After lunch a little aeroplane landed and Wallis and Mutt Summers climbed out; ten minutes later they were with Gibson and Whitworth with a guard on the door. Gibson could not take his beloved Nigger on the raid but could not bear to leave him out altogether, so he gave him the greatest honour he could think of . . . when (or if) the Moehne Dam was breached he would radio back the one code word "Nigger."

In the hangars, messes and barracks the Tannoy came loudly and dramatically to life: "All pilots, navigators and bomb aimers of 617 report to the briefing room immediately." At three o'clock there were some sixty of them in the briefing room on the upper floor of the grey-and-black camouflaged station headquarters. They sat silently on the benches, eyeing the familiar maps, aircraft identification and air-sea rescue posters on the walls, waiting. Whitworth, Gibson and Wallis filed down the centre to the dais and Whitworth nodded to Gibson: "Go ahead, Guy." The room was still.

Gibson faced them, feet braced apart, flushed a little. He had a ruler in one hand, the other in his pocket, and his eyes were bright. He cleared his throat and said:

"You're going to have a chance to clobber the Hun harder than a small force has ever done before." Outside his voice, no sound. "Very soon we are going to attack the major dams in Western Germany." A rustle and murmuring broke the silence—and some deep breaths. They were going to have a sporting chance. Gibson turned to the map and pointed with his ruler.

"Here they are," he said. "Here is the Moehne, here the Eder and here is the Sorpe. As you can see, they are all just east of the Ruhr." He went on to explain the tactics, told each crew what wave they would be on and what dam they were to attack.

Wallis took over and described the dams and what the queer bombs were supposed to do, how success would cripple the Ruhr steel industry, how other factories would be affected and bridges and roads washed away.

Gibson stood up. "Any questions?"

Hopgood said: "I notice, sir, that our route takes us pretty near a synthetic rubber factory at Huls. It's a hot spot. I nearly got the hammer there three months ago. If we go over there low I think it might . . . er . . . upset things."

Gibson looked thoughtfully at the map. Huls was a few miles north of the Ruhr. Satterly and he had known about the Huls flak when they were planning the route but had taken the track as far away from the Ruhr as they could. Better the flak at Huls than the Ruhr.

"If you think it's a bit too close to Huls we'll bring it down a bit," and he pencilled in a wider curve round the little dot. "You'd better all be careful here. The gap isn't too wide. Err on the Huls side if you have to, but watch it you navigators."

He crossed the room to a couple of trestle-tables where three dust covers were hiding something, pulled the covers off, and there were the models of the dams.

"All of you come over and have a look at these," he commanded, and there was a scraping of forms as sixty young men got up and crowded round.

"Look at these till your eyes stick out and you've got every detail photographed on your minds, then go away and draw them from memory, come back and check your drawings, correct them, then go away and draw them again till you're perfect."

They were two hours doing that; each crew concentrated on its own target, working out the best ways in and the best ways out. The known flak guns were marked and they took *very* special note of them. Martin's crew were down for the Moehne

61

with Gibson and Hopgood, and they stood gazing down at the
model.

"What d'you reckon's the best way in?" Leggo asked.

"First thing is to get the final line of attack," Martin said.
"There's the spot!" He put his finger on the tip of a spit
of land running out into the Moehne Lake and ran his finger-
tip in a straight line to the middle of the dam wall, right
between the two towers. It met the wall at right angles. "A
low wide circuit," he said; "come in over the spit and we're
jake."

It was eight o'clock before Gibson was satisfied they knew
it all and said, "Now buzz off and get some grub. But keep
your mouths shut. Not even a whisper to your own crews.
They'll find out tomorrow. If there's one slip and the Hun
gets an inkling you won't be coming back tomorrow night."

They all drank shandy and went to bed, taking little white
pills that the doctor had doled out so they would sleep well.
As Gibson was going along to his room Charles Whitworth
came in looking worried and buttonholed him quietly.

"Guy," he said, "I'm awfully sorry, but Nigger's just been
run over by a car outside the camp. He was killed instan-
taneously."

The car had not even bothered to stop.

Gibson sat a long time on his bed looking at the scratch
marks that Nigger used to make on his door. Nigger and he
had been together since before the war; it seemed to be an
omen.

The morning of May 16 was sunny. Considering the
scurry that went on all day it was remarkable that so few people
at Scampton realised what was happening. Even after the aircraft took off hours later the people watching nearly all thought
it was a special training flight.

It was just after 9 a.m. that Gibson bounced into his office
and told Humphries to draw up the flying programme.

"Training, sir?"—more of a statement than a question.
"No. That is yes—to everyone else," and as Humphries

looked bewildered he said quietly: "We're going to war tonight, but I don't want the world to know. Mark the list 'Night flying programme,' and don't mention the words 'battle order.'"

Watson, the armament chief, was dashing around busily. The pilots were swinging their compasses. Trevor-Roper was seeing that all guns were loaded with full tracer that shot out of the guns at night like angry meteors and to people on the receiving end looked like cannon shells. That was the idea, to frighten the flak gunners and put them off their aim. Each aircraft had two .303 Brownings in the front turret, and four in the tail turret. Each gun fired something like twelve rounds a *second*; each rear turret alone could pump out what looked like forty-eight flaming cannon shells a second; 96,000 rounds lay in the ammunition trays.

Towards noon a Mosquito touched down with the last photos of the dams. The water in the Moehne was 4 feet from the top. After lunch "Gremlin" Matthews, meteorological officer at Grantham, spoke to all the other group met. officers on a locked circuit of trunk lines for half an hour. Such conferences rarely found agreement but this time they did. The lively bespectacled figure of "The Gremlin" walked into Cochrane's office as soon as he had put the receiver down.

"It's all right for tonight, sir." He gave a definite prediction of clear weather over Germany.

"What?" said Cochrane. "No ifs, buts and probablies?" and "The Gremlin" looked mildly cautious just for a moment and took the plunge. "No, sir. It's going to be all right."

Cochrane went out to his car and drove off towards Scampton.

The Tannoy sounded about four o'clock, ordering *all* 617 crews to the briefing room, and soon there were 133 hushed young men sitting on the benches (two crews were out because of illness).

Gibson repeated what he had told the others the previous night, and Wallis, in his earnest, slightly pedantic way, told

63

them about the dams and what their destruction would do.
Cochrane finished with a short, crisp talk.

The final line-up was:

Formation 1: Nine aircraft in three waves, taking off with
ten minutes between waves:

> Gibson,
> Hopgood,
> Martin.

> Young,
> Astell,
> Maltby.

> Maudslay,
> Knight,
> Shannon.

They were to attack the Moehne, and after the Moehne was
breached those who had not bombed would go on to the Eder.

Formation 2: One wave in loose formation:

> McCarthy,
> Byers,
> Barlow,
> Rice,
> Munro.

They were to attack the Sorpe, crossing the coast by the
northern route as a diversion to split the German defences.

Formation 3:

> Townsend,
> Brown,
> Anderson,
> Ottley,
> Burpee.

They would take off later as the mobile reserve.

Supper in the mess was quiet, the calm before the storm.

Above: Gibson and his crew climbing into G for George just before they took off on the dams raid. L. to R.: Trever-Roper, Pulford, Deering, Spafford, Hutchison, Gibson and Taerum.

Below: The Eder Dam breached, photographed by our reconnaissance plane the morning after the attack.

Above: Gibson's crew tell their story at de-briefing after the dams raid. Standing at back: Sir Arthur Harris and Air Vice-Marshal Cochrane. Seated, L. to R: Intelligence Officer, Spafford, Taerum and Trevor-Roper.

Right: The Moehne Dam breached, photographed by our reconnaissance plane the morning after the attack.

No one said much. The non-flying people thought it was to be a training flight, but the crews, who knew it was going to be business—probably sticky—could not say so and there was a faint atmosphere of strain.

With a woman's wit Anne Fowler realised it was to be the real thing. She noticed the crews were having eggs. They often had an egg before a raid, and always after they landed. Most of the others did not notice it, but she started worrying about Shannon.

Dinghy Young said to Gibson, "Can I have your next egg if you don't come back?" But that was the usual chestnut before an "op" and Gibson brushed it aside with a few amiably insulting remarks.

In twos and threes they drifted down to the hangar and started to change. It was not eight o'clock yet; still an hour to take-off and still broad daylight. Martin stuffed his little koala bear into a pocket of his battle-dress jacket and buttoned the flap. It was a grey furry thing about 4 inches high with black button eyes, given to him by his mother as a mascot when the war started. It had as many operational hours as he had.

They drifted over to the grass by the apron and lay in the sun, smoking and quietly talking, waiting. Anne was with Shannon. Fay, the other W.A.A.F. officer, was talking to Martin's crew. Dinghy Young was tidying up his office, just as a matter of course. He had no premonition. Munro seemed half asleep in a deck chair.

Gibson drove up and walked over to Powell.

"Chiefy, I want you to bury Nigger outside my office at midnight. Will you do that?"

"Of course, sir." Powell was startled at the gesture from the hard-bitten Gibson. Gibson did not tell him that he would be about 50 feet over Germany then, not far from the Ruhr. He had it in his mind that he and Nigger might be going into the ground about the same time.

Gibson found himself wishing it were time to go and knew they were all wishing the same. It would be all right once they were in the air. It always was. At ten to nine he said clearly, "Well, chaps, my watch says time to go." Bodies stirred on the grass with elaborate casualness, tossed their parachutes into the flight trucks, climbed in after them, and the trucks moved off round the perimeter track to the hardstandings. Shannon had gone back to the locker room for a moment and when he came out his crew, the only ones left, were waiting impatiently.

The bald-headed Yorkshireman, Jack Buckley, said like a father to his small son, "Have you cleaned your teeth David?" Shannon grinned, hoisted himself elegantly into the flight truck and then they had all gone. Shannon had one of the best crews. Buckley, older than most, of a wealthy family, was his rear gunner and a wild Yorkshireman. Danny Walker was an infallible navigator, a Canadian, dark, quiet and intensely likeable. Sumpter, the bomb aimer, had been a guardsman and was tougher than a prize-fighter. Brian Goodale, the wireless op., was so tall and thin and bent he was known universally as "Concave." And in the air the babyish Shannon was the absolute master, with a scorching tongue when he felt like it.

At exactly ten past nine a red Véry light curled up from Gibson's aircraft, the signal for McCarthy's five aircraft to start; the northern route was longer and they were taking off ten minutes early. Seconds later there was a spurt of blue smoke behind Munro's aircraft as his port inner engine started. One by one the engines came to life. Geoff Rice's engines were turning; Barlow's, then Byers'. The knot of people by the hangar saw a truck rushing at them across the field, and before it came to a stop big McCarthy jumped out and ran at them, roaring like a bull, his red face sweaty, the sandy hair falling over his forehead. In a murderous rage he yelled:

"My aircraft's u/s and there's no deviation card in the spare. Where are those useless instruments jerks!"

The 15-stone Yank had found his own Lancaster, "Q for Queenie," out of action with leaking hydraulics, rushed his crew over to the spare plane, "T for Tom," and found the little card giving the compass deviations missing from it. No hope of accurate flying without it. If McCarthy had met one of the instrument people then he would probably have strangled him.

Chiefy Powell had gone running into the instrument section and found the missing card. He dashed up to McCarthy shouting, "Here it is, sir," and McCarthy grabbed it, well behind schedule now, and turning to run back to the truck, scooped up his parachute from the tarmac where he'd thrown it, but his hand missed the canvas loop handle and he yanked it up by the D-ring of the rip-cord. The pack flaps sprang back in a white blossom as the silk billowed out and trailed after him, and he let out a roar of unbearable fury.

Powell was running for the crew room, but McCarthy snarled, "I'll go without one." He jumped into the truck but before the driver could move off Powell came running up with another parachute, and McCarthy grabbed it through the cabin and shot off across the field. There was a swelling roar from the south side; Munro's Lancaster was rolling, picking up speed, and then it was low in the air, sliding over the north boundary, tucking its wheels up into the big inboard nacelles. Less than a minute later, as McCarthy got to his aircraft, Rice was rolling too, followed by Barlow and Byers.

At precisely 9.25, Gibson in "G for George," Martin in "P for Popsie," and Hopgood, in "M for Mother," punched the buttons of the booster coils and the wisps of blue smoke spurted as the engines whined and spun explosively, first the port inners, the starboard inners, the port outers and the starboard outers. They were going through their cockpit drill while the crews settled at take-off stations, running the engines up to zero boost and testing the magnetoes. A photographer's flash-bulb went off by Gibson's aircraft; Cochrane was there too, standing clear of the slipstream. Fay stood by "P Popsie," waggling her fingers encouragingly at the crew.

"G for George" waddled forward with the shapeless bulk under its belly, taxied to the south fence, swung its long snout to the north and waited, engines turning quietly. ".P Popsie" turned slowly in on the left, and "M Mother" on the right. Gibson rattled out the monotonous orders of his final check.

"Flaps thirty."

Pulford, the engineer, pumped down 30 degrees of flap and repeated, "Flaps thirty."

"Radiators open."

"Radiators open."

"Throttles locked."

Pulford checked the nut on the throttle unit.

"Throttles locked."

"Prepare to take off," Gibson said and checked through to all the crew on the intercom. "O.K., rear gunner?" "O.K." And then all the others. He leaned forward with his thumb up, looking to left and then to right, and Martin and Hopgood raised their thumbs back. Pulford closed his hand over the four throttles and pushed till the engines deepened their note and the aircraft was throbbing . . . straining; then Gibson flicked his brakes off, there was the hiss of compressed air and they were rolling, all three of them, engineers sliding the throttles right forward.

The blare of twelve engines slammed over the field and echoed in the hangar, the tails slowly came up as they picked up speed in a loose vic, ungainly with nearly 5 tons of bomb and over 5 tons of petrol each. Gibson held her down for a long time and the a.s.i. was flicking on 110 m.p.h. before he tightened back on the wheel and let her come unstuck after a long, slow bounce. At 200 feet they turned slowly on course with the sun low behind.

McCarthy eased "T for Tom" off the runway twenty minutes late and set course on his own. At 9.47 Dinghy Young led Astell and Maltby off. Eight minutes after that Maudslay, Shannon and Knight were in the air. Anne waved them off. The final five, the reserve aircraft, did not take off till two hours later. By the time they arrived in the target area Gibson, if still alive, would know where to send them.

CHAPTER VII

ATTACK

GIBSON slid over the Wash at a hundred feet. The cockpit was hot and he was flying in his shirtsleeves with Mae West over the top; after a while he yelled, "Hey, Hutch, turn the heat off."

"Thank God for that," the wireless operator said, screwing the valve shut. The heat in a Lancaster runs down the fuselage but comes out round the wireless operators' seat, so he is always too hot, while the rear gunner is always too cold.

The sun astern on the quarter threw long shadows on fields peaceful and fresh with spring crops; dead ahead the moon was swimming out of the ground haze like a bullseye. Gibson flew automatically, eyes flicking from the horizon to the a.s.i., to the repeater compass in its rubber suspension.

The haze of Norfolk passed a few miles to port. In the nose, Spafford said, "There's the sea," and a minute later they were low over Southwold, the shingle was beneath them, and then they were over the water, flat and grey in the evening light. England faded behind. "G George" dropped down to 50 feet, and on each side Martin and Hopgood came down too, putting off the evil moment when German radar would pick them up. You couldn't put it off indefinitely; about twenty miles from the Dutch coast the blips would be flicking on the radar screens and the orders would be going out to the flak batteries and fighter fields.

Martin ranged up alongside and there was a light winking as he flashed his Aldis lamp at them.

"What's he saying, Hutch?" Gibson asked.

"We're going to get screechers tomorrow night." Hutchinson

picked up his own Aldis and winked back, "You're darned right. Biggest binge of all time." Hutchinson didn't drink.

Terry Taerum, Gibson's navigator, spoke: "Our ground speed is exactly 203½ miles an hour. We will be there in exactly one hour, ten minutes and thirty seconds. We ought to cross the coast dead on track. Incidentally, you're one degree off course." The last part was the standing joke. The pilot who can fly without sometimes yawing a degree or so off course has yet to be born.

In the ops. room of 5 Group H.Q. at Grantham, Cochrane was walking Barnes Wallis up and down, trying to comfort him. Wallis was fidgety and jittery, and Cochrane was talking of anything but the bomb, trying to get Wallis's mind off it, but Wallis could think of nothing else.

"Just think what a wonderful job you made of the Wellington," Cochrane said encouragingly. "It's a magnificent machine; been our mainstay for over three years."

"Oh dear, no," lamented the disconcerting scientist. "Do you know, every time I pass one I wonder how I could ever have designed anything so crude."

A black Bentley rushed up the gravelled drive outside, pulled up by the door and the sentries snapped rigidly to attention as Harris himself jumped briskly out. He came into the ops. room. "How's it going, Cocky?"

"All right so far, sir," Cochrane said. "Nothing to report yet." They walked up and down the long room between the wall where the aircraft blackboards were and the long desks that ran down the other side, where men were sitting. Satterly was there, "The Gremlin," the intelligence man and Dunn, chief signals officer, sitting by a telephone plugged in to the radio in the signals cabin outside. He would get all the Morse from the aircraft there; it was too far for low-flying planes to get through by ordinary speech.

Harris and Cochrane talked quietly, and Wallis was walking miserably with them but not talking, breaking away every now and then to look at the big operations map on the end wall. The track lines had been pencilled in and he was counting off the miles they should be travelling. It was 10.35 when Cochrane looked at his watch and said, "They ought to be coming up to the Dutch coast now."

The sun had gone and the moon was inching higher into the dusk, lighting a road ahead across the water; outside the dancing road the water was hardly visible, a dark mass with a couple of little flecks.

Taerum said, "Five minutes to the Dutch coast," and the crew snapped out of the wordless lull of the past half hour. "Good," Gibson said. Martin and Hopgood eased their aircraft forward till the black snouts nosed alongside Gibson and veered out to make a wider target, their engines snarling thinly in gusts above the monotonous roar in "G George." Flying so low, just off the water, they seemed to be sliding very fast along the moonpath towards the waiting flak.

Spafford said, "There's the coast." It was a black line lying dim and low on the water, and then from a couple of miles out on the port side a chain of glowing little balls was climbing into the sky. "Flak ship," said Martin laconically. The shells were way off and he ignored them. The sparkling moonpath ended abruptly, they tore across the white line of surf and were over enemy territory. "New course 105 magnetic," Taerum called, and the three aircraft swung gently to the left as they started the game of threading their way through the flak.

The northern wave made landfall about the same time, sighting Vlieland and turning south-east to cut across the narrow part and down over the Zuyder Zee. Munro led them across the dark spit; it was so narrow they would see the water again in about thirty seconds and have another seventy miles of comparatively safe water, but without warning there were flashes below and up came the fiery little balls. Munro felt the shock as they hit the aircraft, and then they were past and over the water again. Munro called on the intercom, to see if the crew were all right, but the earphones were dead.

Pigeon, the wireless op., was standing by his shoulder shouting into his ear, "No radio. No intercom. Flak's smashed it. I think everyone's O.K." Munro flew on several miles, trying to fool himself they could still carry on, but it was no good and he knew it. Without radio he could not direct the attack on the Sorpe; could not even direct his own crew or get bombing instructions. Swearing, he turned for home.

Inside the Zuyder the water was dark and quite flat, treacherously deceptive for judging height. Geoff Rice slipped down a little to level at 60 feet by his belly lights, but the lights were not working properly and lured him lower as he tried to get a fix. A hammer seemed to hit the aircraft like a bolt and there was a tearing roar above the engines. Rice dragged her off the water, but the belly was torn out of her and the bomb had gone with it. The gutted fuselage had scooped up a couple of tons of water; it was pouring out of her and the rear gunner was nearly drowning in his turret. Marvellously she still flew but was dropping back, and when they found the bomb was gone Rice turned her heavily back towards England.

The remaining two, Barlow and Byers, skirted their pinpoint on the cape at Stavoren and ten minutes later crossed to the enemy land again at Harderwijk. No one knows exactly how soon it was that the flak came curling up at them again, but there is a report that as Barlow's aircraft hit the ground the bomb went off with a blinding flash, lighting the countryside like a rising sun for ten seconds before it died and left nothing. It was either then or soon after that Byers and his crew died too. Nothing more was heard from him. Only McCarthy was left of the Sorpe team, flying sixty miles behind, and perhaps that is what saved him.

Over Holland, Gibson, Martin and Hopgood were down as low as 40 feet, playing hide-and-seek with the ground, the bomb aimers calling terse warnings as houses and trees loomed up, and the aircraft skimmed over them. They were cruising fast and under the cowlings the exhaust manifolds were glowing. Once the three pulled up fast as the pylons of a power line rushed at them, and they just cleared the wires.

Four miles to port they saw the flare-path of Gilze-Rijen, German night-fighter field, and a few miles farther on they passed just to the left of the night-fighter aerodrome at Eindhoven. They could expect night fighters now; the ops. rooms for miles around must be buzzing. Martin and Hopgood closed in on each side of Gibson for mutual protection. They should be able to see any fighter coming in because he would be higher, while they, low against the dark ground, would be hard to see, and that was their strength. Also their weakness where the flak was concerned. Their aircraft were higher, outlined. Just past Eindhoven, Gibson led them in a gentle turn to the north-east on the new course that would take them round the bristling guns of the Ruhr.

A few miles back the other two vics of three were on course too. Dinghy Young pin-pointed over the canal at Rosendaal and turned delicately to take them between the fighter fields, but Bill Astell did not seem sure this was the exact turning point. He bore off a little to the south for a minute and then turned back, but had fallen half a mile behind and was a fraction off track. They did not see him again, and it must have been quite soon after that the flak or fighter, whatever it was, got him.

Fourteen left.

The leading three slid across the border into Germany and saw no light or movements anywhere, only darkness filled with the beat of engines. Taerum thought they were south of track, so they edged to the north, a little nervily because this was the treacherous leg; they were coming up to the Rhine to sneak between the forewarned guns of Huls and the Ruhr. Just short of the river some twelve light flak guns opened up without warning; the aircraft gunners squirted back at the roots of the tracer and then they were out of range. No one badly hit. The Rhine was rushing at them and up from a

73

barge spat a thin line of tracer, but they were past before the bullets found them.

Two minutes later more guns opened up, and this time three searchlights lit on Gibson. Foxlee and Deering were shooting at the searchlights. One of them popped out but the two others held, and the air was full of tracer. The rear gunners came into action, the searchlights switched to Martin, blinding him, and Gibson could read the big P on the side of the Lancaster. Every gun was firing, the aircraft juddering with the recoil, and then they were through with throttles wide.

Ahead and just to the left another searchlight sprang to life and caught Gibson. Foxlee was firing instantly, holding his triggers in a long burst, his tracer whipping into the light. It flicked out, and as they went over in the dying glow they saw the gunners scattering. Tammy Simpson opened up from the rear turret till they were out of range. You can't take prisoners in an aircraft.

They were past and shook themselves back into formation. Hutchinson tapped out a flak warning, giving the exact position, and way back in Grantham, Dunn picked it up and the powerful group radio re-broadcast it at full strength to all other aircraft.

Gibson swung them north around Hamm, whose marshalling yards will for years be notorious. Taerum said, "New course, skipper, 165 magnetic," and then they were hugging the ground on the last leg, slicing between Soest and Werl. Now the moon was high enough to light the ground and ahead loomed the dark hills that cradled the water. They climbed to the ridge that rimmed the horizon, crossed into the valley, and down below lay the flat sheet of Moehne Lake.

It was like looking down on the model: the same saucer of water, the same dim fields and across the neck of the lake the squat rampart hugging the water, crowned by the towers. In the half-light it looked like a battleship, but more impregnable. Reinforced concrete a hundred feet thick.

The dam came suddenly to life, prickling with sharp flashes, and the lines of angry red meteors were streaming into the sky and moving about blindly as the gunners hosed the area.

"Bit aggressive, aren't they?" said Trevor-Roper. The pilots swung the aircraft away and headed in wide circles round the lake, keeping out of range and waiting for the others. There seemed to be about ten guns, some in the fields on each side of the lake near the dam, and some—a lot—in the towers in the dam.

Gibson started calling the other aircraft, and one by one they reported, except Astell. He called Astell again at the end, but Astell had been dead for an hour. After a while Gibson gave up and said soberly over the intercom., "Well, boys, I suppose we'd better start the ball rolling." It was the end of the waiting and the start of action, when thought is submerged. He flicked his transmitter switch:

"Hello all Cooler aircraft, I am going in to attack. Stand by to come in in your order when I tell you. Hello 'M Mother.' Stand by to take over if anything happens."

"O.K. Leader. Good luck." Hopgood's voice was a careful monotone.

Gibson turned wide, hugging the hills at the eastern end of the lake. Pulford had eased the throttles on and she was roaring harshly, picking up speed and quivering, the nose slowly coming round till three miles ahead they saw the towers and the rampart of the dam, and in between, the flat dark water. Spafford said, "Good show. This is wizard. I can see everything." They came out of the hills and slammed across the water, touching 240 now, and Gibson rattled off the last orders:

"Check height, Terry! Speed control, Pulford! Gunners ready! Coming up, Spam!" Taerum flicked the belly lights on and, peering down from the blister, started droning: "Down . . . down . . . down . . . up a bit . . . steady, stead-y-y." The lights were touching each other, "G George" was exactly at 60 feet and the flak gunners had seen the lights. The streams of glowing shells were swivelling and lowering, and then the shells were whipping towards them, seeming to move

75

slowly at first like all flak, and then rushing madly at their eyes as the aircraft plunged into them.

Gibson held her steady, pointing between the towers. Taerum was watching out of the blister, Pulford had a hand on the throttles and his eyes on the a.s.i., Spafford held the plywood sight to his eye and the towers were closing in on the nails. Gibson shouted to Pulford, "Stand by to pull me out of the seat if I get hit!" There was a sudden snarling clatter up in the nose; Deering had opened up, his tracer spitting at the towers.

The dam was a rushing giant, darkness split with flashes, the cockpit stank of cordite and thought was nothing but a cold alarm shouting, "In another minute we shall be dead," and then Spafford screamed, "Bomb gone!" loud and sharp. Seconds later they rocketed over the dam between the towers. A red Véry light soared up as Hutchinson pulled the trigger to let the others know, and then the deeper snarling chatter as Trevor-Roper opened up on the towers from the rear.

It was over and memory was confusion as they cork-screwed down the valley, hugging the dark earth sightless to the flak. They were out of range and Gibson lifted her out of the hills, turning steeply, and looked back. A voice in his earphones said, "Good show, Leader, Nice work."

The black water between the towers suddenly rose and split and a huge white core erupted through the middle and climbed towards the sky. The lake was writhing, and as the white column reached its peak and hung a thousand feet high, like a ghost against the moon, the heavy explosion reached the aircraft. They looked in awe as they flew back to one side and saw sheets of water spilling over the dam and thought for a wild moment it had burst. The fury of the water passed and the dam was still there, the white column slowly dying.

Round the lake they flew while Hutchinson tapped out in code to base. In a few minutes Gibson thought the lake was calm enough for the next bomb and called:

"Hello 'M Mother.' You may attack now. Good luck."

"O.K. Leader. Attacking." Hopgood was still carefully laconic. He was lost in the darkness over the hills at the end of the lake while the others waited. They saw his bellylights flick on and the two little yellow pools sliding over the water closing and joining as he found his height. He was straight and level on his run; the flak saw him and the venomous fire-flies were darting at him. He plunged on; the gap was closing fast when the shells found him and someone said, "He's been hit!"

A red glow was blossoming round the inner port wing tank, and then a long, long ribbon of flame trailed behind "M Mother." The bomb aimer must have been hit, because the bomb overshot the parapet on to the power house below.

"M Mother" was past the dam, nose up, straining for height so the crew could bale out, when the tanks blew up with an orange flare, a wing ripped away and the bomber spun to the ground in burning, bouncing pieces. The bomb went off near the power house like a brilliant sun. It was all over in seconds.

A voice said over the R/T, "Poor old Hoppy."

Gibson called up: "Hello 'P Popsie.' Are you ready?"

"O.K. Leader. Going in."

"I'll fly across the dam as you make your run and try and draw the flak off you."

"O.K. Thanks, Leader."

Martin was turning in from the hills and Gibson headed across the lake, parallel to the dam and just out of effective range of the guns. As Martin's spotlights merged and sped across the water Gibson back-tracked and Deering and Trevor-Roper opened up; six lines of tracer converged on the towers, drawing their attention, so that for some seconds most of the guns did not notice Martin rocketing over the water. He held his height and Whittaker had the speed right. They were tracking straight for the middle of the dam between the moon-bathed towers when the gunners spotted them and threw a curtain of fire between the towers, spreading like a fan so they would have to fly through it. Martin drove straight ahead.

Two guns swung at them, and as the shells whipped across the water sharp-eyed little Foxlee was yelling as he squirted back, his tracer lacing and tangling with the flak.

A sharp "Bomb gone!" from Bob Hay, and in the same instant a shudder as two shells smacked into the starboard wing, one of them exploding in the inner petrol tank. A split second of flashes as they shot through the barrage. Tammy Simpson opened up from the rear turret, Chambers shot the Véry light and they were down the valley. Whittaker was looking fearfully at the hole in the starboard wing, but no fire was coming. He suddenly realised why and nudged Martin, yelling in his ear, "The starboard tank was empty!"

Martin shouted, "Bomb gone, Leader."

"O.K. 'P Popsie.' Let me know when you're out of the flak. Hello 'A Apple.' Are you ready?"

"O.K. Leader."

"Right. Go ahead. Let me know when you're in position and I'll draw the flak for you."

Martin called again "'P Popsie' clear now, Leader."

"O.K. Are you hit?"

"Yeah. Starboard wing, but we're all right. We can make it."

The lake suddenly boiled again by the dam and spewed out the great white column that climbed again to a thousand feet. More water was cascading over the dam, but it cleared soon and the dam was still there.

Dinghy Young was on the air again. "'A Apple' making bombing run."

Gibson headed back over the lake where his gunners could play with fire, and this time Martin did the same. As Young came plunging across the lake Gibson and Martin came in on each side, higher up, and the flak did not know where to shoot. Young swept past the dam and reported he was all right. The great explosion was up against the dam wall again, beautifully accurate, but the dam was still there, and again Gibson waited till the plume of spray had cleared and the water was calm.

He called Maltby and ordered him in, and as Maltby came across the water Gibson and Martin came in with him, firing with every gun that could bear and flicking the navigation lights on this time to help the flak gunners shoot at the wrong target. The red cartridge soared up from Maltby's aircraft to signal "Attack successful."

In a few moments the mountain of water erupted skyward again under the dam wall. It was uncanny how accurate the bomb was. The spray from the explosions was misting up the whole valley now and it was hard to see what was happening by the dam. Gibson called Shannon to make his attack, and the words were barely out of his mouth when a sharp voice filled his earphones:

"It's gone! It's gone! Look at it!" Wheeling round the valley side Martin had seen the concrete face abruptly split and crumble under the weight of water. Gibson swung in close and was staggered. A ragged hole 100 yards across and 100 feet deep split the dam and the lake was pouring out of it, 134 million tons of water crashing into the valley in a jet 200 feet long, smooth on top, foaming at the sides where it tore at the rough edges of the breach and boiling over the scarred earth where the power house had been.

Gibson told Shannon to "skip it."

The others flew over and were awed into silence. In the moonglow they watched a wall of water rolling down the valley, 25 feet high, moving 20 feet a second. A gunner still on his feet in one of the towers opened up at them until lines of tracer converged on the root of the flak and it stopped abruptly. The awed silence was broken by a babble of intercom. chatter as they went mad with excitement; the only man not looking being Hutchinson, sitting at his keyboard tapping out "Nigger."

Soon the hissing steam and spray blurred the valley. Gibson called Martin and Maltby to set course for home, and told Young, Shannon, Maudslay and Knight to follow him east to the Eder. Young was to control if Gibson was shot down.

CHAPTER VIII

THE WRITHING LAKE

AT Grantham a long silence had followed the flak warning at Huls, and then Dunn's phone rang sharply, and in the dead silence they all heard the Morse crackling in the receiver. It was quite slow and Cochrane, bending near, could read it. "Goner," he said. "From G George." "Goner" was the code word that meant Gibson had exploded his bomb in the right place.

"I'd hoped one bomb might do it," Wallis said gloomily.

"It's probably weakened it," Cochrane soothed him. Harris looked non-committal. There was no more from "G George," and they went on walking. A long silence. Nothing came through when Hopgood crashed. The phone rang, "Goner" from "P Popsie." Another dragging silence. "Goner" from "A Apple." Wallis swears even today that there was half an hour between each signal, but the log shows only about five minutes. "Goner" from "J Johnny." That was Maltby, and the aura of gloom settled deeper over Wallis.

A minute later the phone rang again and the Morse crackled so fast the others could not read it. Dunn printed it letter by letter on a signals pad and let out a cry, "Nigger. It's Nigger. It's gone."

Wallis threw his arms over his head and went dancing round the room. The austere face of Cochrane cracked into a grin, he grabbed one of Wallis's hands and started congratulating him. Harris, with the first grin on his face that Wallis had ever seen, grabbed the other hand and said:

"Wallis, I didn't believe a word you said about this bomb, but you could sell me a pink elephant now."

The moment in which H.M. King George VI selected 617 Squadron's badge. *L. to R.*: Air Vice-Marshal Cochrane, Gibson, H.M. King George VI and Charles Whitworth. In the foreground is a model of the Moehne Dam.

Above : One of the most remarkable photographs of the war—the moment at which Cheshire dropped his incendiary markers on the factory at Limoges. The incendiaries are showering over the factory roofs and, top-left centre, is the tailwheel of Cheshire's Lancaster.

Below : The remarkable bombing of the Michelin factory at Clermont-Ferrand, when they were told to hit the two factory workshops and leave the canteen. Centre: the two factory buildings destroyed, and lower right, the large canteen, undamaged.

He said, a little later when some of the excitement had died down: "I must tell Portal immediately." Sir Charles Portal, Chief of the R.A.F., was in Washington that night on a mission, actually at that moment dining with Roosevelt. Harris picked up the nearest phone and said, "Get me the White House."

The little W.A.A.F. on the switchboard knew nothing of the highly secret raid. Even at Grantham, Cochrane's security had been perfect. She did not realise the importance of it all, or the identity of the great man who was speaking, and was caught off guard. "Yes, sir," she said automatically and, so they say, dialled the only White House she knew, a jolly little roadhouse a few miles out of Grantham.

Harris must have thought she was a very smart operator when the White House answered so quickly, and there are reported to have been moments of incredible and indescribable comedy as Harris asked for Portal, and the drowsy landlord, testy at being hauled out of bed after midnight, told him in well-chosen words he didn't have anyone called Portal staying at the place; in fact, he didn't have anyone staying at all, because he didn't have room, and if he did have room he would not have anyone staying there who had people who called him up at that time of night. Not for long anyway.

Harris went red, and there were some explosive exchanges before one of them slammed the receiver down. Someone slipped down and had a word with the little W.A.A.F., and she tried in terror for the next hour to raise Washington, but without success.

Three kilometres down the valley from the Moehne lay the sleeping village of Himmelpforten, which means Gate of Heaven. The explosions had wakened the village priest, Father Berkenkopf, and he guessed instantly what was happening; he had been afraid of it for three years. He ran to his small stone church, Porta Coeli (which also means Gate of Heaven—in Latin) and begun tugging grimly on the bell-rope, the signal he had arranged with his villagers. It is not certain how many were warned in time. In the darkness the clanging of the bell rolled ominously round the valley and then it was muffled in the thunder moving nearer. Berkenkopf must have heard it and known what it meant, but it seems that he was still pulling at the bell when the flood crushed the church and the village of the Gate of Heaven and rolled them down the valley.

It went for many miles and took more villages, a tumbling maelstrom of water and splintered houses, beds and frying-pans, the chalice from Porta Coeli and the bell, the bodies of cattle and horses, pigs and dogs, and the bodies of Father Berkenkopf and other human beings.

War, as someone said, is a great leveller, but he did not mean it quite as literally or as bitterly as this.

The Eder was hard to find because fog was filling the valley. Gibson circled it for some time before he was certain he was there. One by one the others found it and soon they were all in a left-hand circuit round the lake. There was no flak; probably the Germans thought the Eder did not need it. It lay deep in a fold of the hills; the ridges around were a thousand feet high and it was no place to dive a heavy aircraft at night.

Gibson said, "O.K. Dave. Start your attack."

Shannon flew a wide circuit over the ridges and then put his nose right down, but the dive was not steep enough and he overshot. Sergeant Henderson slammed on full throttle, and Shannon hauled back on the stick and they just cleared the mountain on the far side.

"Sorry Leader," Shannon said a little breathlessly. "Made a mess of that. I'll try it again."

Five times more he dived into the dark valley but he failed every time to get into position and nearly stood the Lancaster on her tail to get out of the hills again. He called up finally, "I think I'd better circle and try to get to know this place."

"O.K. Dave. You hang around a bit and let someone else have a crack. Hullo 'Z Zebra.' You have a go now."

Maudslay acknowledged and a minute later was diving down

the contour of the hills, only to overshoot and go rocketing up again like Shannon. He tried again but the same thing happened. Maudslay said he was going to try once more. He came slowly over the ridges, turned in the last moment and the nose dropped sharply into the gloom as he forced her down into the valley. They saw him level out very fast, and then the spotlights flicked on to the water and closed quickly and he was tracking for the dam. His red Véry light curled up as Fuller called "Bombs gone!"

But something went wrong. The bomb hit the parapet of the dam at high speed and blew up on impact with a tremendous flash; in the glare they saw "Z Zebra" for a moment just above the explosion. Then only blackness.

Gibson said painfully, knowing it was useless:

"Henry, Henry—hullo 'Z Zebra,' are you all right?" There was no answer. He called again and, incredibly, out of the darkness a very faint voice said, "I think so . . . stand by," They all heard it, Gibson and Shannon and Knight, and wondered that it was possible. After a while Gibson called again but there was no answer. Maudslay never came back.

Gibson called, "O.K., David, will you attack now?"

Shannon tried and missed again; came round once more, plunged into the darkness and this time made it, curling out of the dive at the foot of the lake and tracking for the dam. He found his height quickly, the bomb dropped clear and Shannon roughly pulled his plane up over the shoulder of the mountain. Under the parapet the bomb spewed up the familiar plume of white water and as it drifted down Gibson, diving over the lake, saw that the dam was still there. There was only Knight left. He had the last bomb. Gibson ordered him in.

Knight tried once and couldn't make it. He tried again. Failed. "Come in down moon and dive for the point, Les," Shannon said. He gave more advice over the R/T, and Knight listened quietly. He was a young Australian who did not drink, his idea of a riotous evening being to write letters home and go to the pictures. He dived to try again, made a perfect run and they saw the splashes as his bomb skipped over the water in feathers of spray. Seconds later the water erupted, and as Gibson slanted down to have a look he saw the wall of the dam burst open and the torrent come crashing out.

This was even more fantastic than the Moehne. The breach in the dam was as big and there were over 200 million tons of water pouring through. The Eder Valley was steeper and they watched speechlessly as the flood foamed and tossed down the valley, lengthening like a snake. It must have been rolling at 30 feet a second. They saw a car in front racing to get clear; only the lights they saw, like two frightened eyes spearing the dark, and the car was not fast enough. The foam crawled up on it, the headlights turned opalescent green as the water rolled over, and suddenly they flicked out.

Hutchison was tapping "Dinghy" in Morse; that was the code to say that the Eder was destroyed. When he had finished Gibson called, "O.K. all Cooler aircraft. You've had your look. Let's go home." and the sound of their engines died over the hills as they flew west to fight their way back.

McCarthy had fought a lone way through to the Sorpe, tucked down in rolling hills south of the Moehne. The valleys were full of mist, so it was a long time before he pin-pointed himself over the lake, dimly seeing through the haze a shape he recognised from the model.

He tried a dummy run and found, as the others found before at the Eder, that there was a hill at each end so that he would have to dive steeply, find his aiming point quickly and pull up in a hurry. He tried twice more but was not satisfied and came in a third time, plunging through the mist trying to see through the suffused moonlight. He nearly hit the water and levelled out very low. Johnson picked up the aiming point and seconds later yelled, "Bomb gone!" and they were climbing up over the far hills when the bomb exploded by the dam wall. McCarthy dived back over the dam and they saw that the crest had crumbled for 50 yards. As they turned on course for England,

Eaton tapped out the code word that told of their successful drop.

Wallis's joy was complete. Cochrane radioed "G George." asking if he had any aircraft left to divert to the Sorpe, and Hutchinson answered, "None." Satterly, who had been plotting the path of the reserve force by dead reckoning, radioed orders to them.

Burpee, in "S Sugar," was directed to the Sorpe, but he did not answer. They called again and again, but there was only silence. He was dead.

Brown, in "F Freddy," was sent to the Sorpe and reached it after McCarthy had left; the mist was swirling thicker and, though he dived low over the dam, Oancia, the bomb aimer, could not pick it up in time.

Brown dived back on a second run but Oancia still found the mist foiled him. They tried eight times, and then Brown pulled up and they had a conference over the intercom. On the next run Oancia dropped a cluster of incendiaries in the woods to the side of the dam. They burned dazzlingly and the trees caught too, so that on the tenth run Oancia picked up the glare a long way back, knew exactly where the target was and dropped his load accurately.

They pulled round in a climbing turn and a jet of water and rubble climbed out of the mist and hung against the moon; down in the mist itself they saw a shock wave of air like a giant smoke ring circling the base of the spout.

Anderson, in "Y Yorker," was also sent to the Sorpe, but he was still later than Brown, and now the valley was completely under mist so that the lake and the dam were hidden and he had to turn back with his bomb.

Ottley, in "C Charlie," was ordered to the Lister Dam, one of the secondary targets. He acknowledged "Message received," but that was the last anyone ever heard from him.

The last man was Townsend, in "O Orange," and his target was the Ennerpe. He searched a long time before he found it in the mist, and made three runs before he was satisfied and dropped the bomb.   It was accurate.

Ten out of the nineteen were coming home, hugging the ground, 8 tons lighter now in bomb and petrol load and travelling at maximum cruising, about 245, not worrying about petrol; only about getting home.   The coast was an hour away and the sun less than that.   They knew the fighters were overhead waiting for a lightening sky in the east.

Gibson saw the dark blotch of Hamm ahead and swung to the east.   To the left he saw another aircraft; it was going too near Hamm, he thought, whoever it was, and then the flak came up and something was burning in the sky where the aircraft had been.   It was falling, hit like a shooting star and blew up.   It may have been Burpee.   Or Ottley.

Townsend was the last away from the dams area.   He flew back over the Moehne and could not recognise it at first; the lake had changed shape.   Already there were mudbanks with little boats stranded on them, and bridges stood long-legged out of the shrinking water.   The torpedo net had vanished, and below the dam the country was different.   There was a new lake where no lake had been; a strange lake, writhing down the valley.

Miraculously most of them dodged the flak on the way back; lucky this, because dawn was coming, the sky was paler in the east and at 50 feet the aircraft were sitting ducks.   In Gibson's aircraft Trevor-Roper called on the intercom., "Unidentified enemy aircraft behind."

"O.K., Trev."   "G George" sank till it was scraping the fields and they could see the startled cattle running in panic. Trevor-Roper said, "O.K., we've lost him," but Gibson still kept down on the deck.

Over Holland he called Dinghy Young, but there was no answer and he wondered what had happened to him.   (Group knew!   They had got a brief message from Young.   He had come over the coast a little high and the last squirts of flak had hit him. He had struggled on a few more miles, losing height, and then ditched in the water.)

Coming to the West Wall, Gibson climbed to about 300 feet, Pulford slid the throttles right forward and they dived to the ground again, picking up speed, and at 270 m.p.h. they roared over the tank traps and the naked sand and then they were over the grey morning water and beyond the flak.

Ten minutes later it was daylight over Holland, and Townsend was still picking his way out. He was lucky and went between the guns.

Maltby was first back, landing in the dawn and finding the whole station had been waiting up since dusk. Harris, Cochrane and Wallis met him at the hardstanding and he told them what he had seen. Martin landed. Mutt Summers went out to meet him and found Martin under the aircraft looking at a ragged hole in his wing.

One by one they landed and were driven to the ops. room, where Harris, Cochrane and Wallis listened intently. Gibson came in, his hair pressed flat from eight hours under his helmet. "It was a wizard party, sir," he said. "Went like a bomb, but we couldn't quieten some of the flak. I'm afraid some of the boys got the hammer. Don't know how many yet. Hopgood and Maudslay for certain."

They had bacon and egg and stood round the bar with pints, drinking and waiting for the others. It was an hour since the last aircraft had landed. Shannon said Dinghy Young had ditched, and someone said, "What, is the old soak going to paddle back again? That's the third time he's done it. He'll do it once too often." Young *had* done it once too often. He was not in his dinghy this time.

Wallis was asking anxiously, "Where are they? Where are all the others?"

Summers said, "Oh, they'll be along. Give 'em time. They've probably landed somewhere else": but after a while it was impossible to cover up any longer and Wallis knew they were all standing round getting drunk for the ones who were not coming back. Except himself; he didn't drink. Martin made him take a half pint but he only held it and stood there blinking back tears and said, "Oh, if I'd only known, I'd never have started this!" Mutt and Charles Whitworth tried to take his mind off it.

Gibson left the party early, but not for bed; he went over to the hangar to give Humphries and Chiefy Powell a hand with the casualty telegrams to the next of kin. Fifty-six beardless men out of 133 were missing, and only three had got out by parachute at a perilously low height to spend the rest of the war miserably in prison camp. Gibson had expected to lose several over the Moehne, where those sinister installations had been spotted by the recce aircraft, but they had lost only one there. (It was not till after the war that they discovered that those dark shapes on top of the Moehne had been—trees . . . ornamental pine trees. In the middle of the war the Germans would not send extra guns but had gone to the trouble of decorating it.)

Around lunchtime the party survivors transferred to Whitworth's house and Whitworth's best port. Wallis came tiredly downstairs in a dressing-gown, distressed about the losses, and after a while he left to fly back to Weybridge with Summers. Martin gave him a sleeping-pill as he was leaving so he would sleep that night. He slept all right. The weary scientist swallowed the pill sitting up in bed at home and went out like a light.

About two o'clock even the durable Martin and Whittaker were ready for bed, but they were all up again at five o'clock and drove over in buses to a party at Woodhall Spa. On the way back David Shannon and Anne were sitting close together, and Shannon leaned closer so the others couldn't hear and asked her to marry him.

"Oh, David," she said, and there was a pause, "n-n-not with that moustache."

Shannon fingered the growth defensively. It was a dear possession; made him look years older—at least twenty-two. He groaned. "What is it?" he said. "My moustache or you?" There was only silence and he sighed, "All right, I'll whip it off."

In the morning 617 Squadron went on leave, three days for the ground crew, seven days for the aircrew survivors—except Gibson, who stayed on two days to write to the mothers of the dead. He wrote them all out in his own hand, different ones each time, fifty-six of them.

In London and in their homes the crews found they were famous, though the headlines in Germany were not so flattering. A recce Mosquito arrived back from over Germany with the first pictures of the damage, and they were breath-taking. The Moehne and Eder lakes were empty and 330 million tons of water were spreading like a cancer through the western Ruhr valleys, the bones of towns and villages showing lifeless in the wilderness.

The Ruhr, which had been enduring its ordeal by fire, was having it now by water. For fifty miles from the Moehne and fifty miles from the Eder coal mines were flooded and factories collapsed. At Fritzlar one of Hitler's largest military aerodromes was under water, the aircraft, the landing ground, hangars, barracks and bomb dumps. Roads, railways and bridges had disappeared. The Unterneustadt industrial suburb of Kassel, forty miles from the Eder, was under water, and the flood ran miles on down the Fulda Valley. Canal banks were washed away, power stations had disappeared, the Ruhr foundries were without water for making steel. A dozen waterworks were destroyed as far away as Gelsenkirchen, Dortmund, Hamm and Bochum. The communications system feeding raw materials to the Ruhr and taking away the finished weapons was disrupted. Some factories were not swept away but still could not work because there was no electricity. Or no water.

In the small town of Neheim alone 2,000 men, including 1,250 soldiers, were diverted to repair damage. Another 2,000 men were trying to repair the dams. And in the months ahead, in the

Battle of the Ruhr, there was not enough water to put the fires out.

The official German report said it was "a dark picture of destruction." By the next autumn they might know how much industrial production would be ultimately affected, but estimated it was going to mean the equivalent of the loss of production of 100,000 men for several months.

A hundred and twenty-five factories were either destroyed or badly damaged, nearly 3,000 hectares of arable land were ruined, 25 bridges had vanished, and 21 more were badly damaged. The livestock losses were 6,500 cattle and pigs.

There was a moral price to pay too; there always is. 1,294 people drowned in the floods, and most were civilians. Most were not German—there were 749 slaves and prisoners among the dead. There had been a Russian P.o.W. camp in the valley below the Eder.

Gibson spent his leave quietly with his wife, Eve, who had had a shock when she had opened the papers and found Guy's name and photographs splashed over the front pages. All the time he had been at 617 he had told her he was having a rest at a flying training school.

Micky Martin was summoned to Australian Air Force Headquarters, where a dark, pretty girl called Wendy tried her hardest to get him to talk about the raid for a story for Australia, but all the incorrigible Martin would say was, "Come and have lunch with me," and kept it up until she did.

Then the decorations came through—thirty-three of them. Gibson was awarded the Victoria Cross. Martin, McCarthy, Maltby, Shannon and Knight got D.S.Os. Bob Hay, Hutchison, Leggo and Danny Walker got bars to their D.F.Cs. There were ten D.F.Cs., among them Trevor-Roper, Buckley, Deering, Spafford and Taerum. Brown and Townsend got the Conspicuous Gallantry Medal, and there were twelve D.F.Ms., among them being Tammy Simpson, Sumpter, Oancia and Pulford.

When he heard the news Gibson rang for Flight Sergeant Powell. "Chiefy," he said quietly, "if I ever change, tell me."

On May 27 the King and Queen visited the newly famous squadron, and the crews pressed their uniforms and stood in front of their aircraft to be presented, though Martin overlooked one point and was standing there smartly to attention with an orange sticking out of his pocket.

Gibson had had a competition for a design for a squadron badge, and after the parade he showed the King the roughs and asked if he would choose one. The King called the Queen, and unanimously they picked a drawing showing a dam breached in the middle with water flowing out and bolts of lightning above. Underneath, the motto was "*Apres nous, le déluge.*"

CHAPTER IX

THE BLACKEST HOUR

WEEKS passed placidly. The squadron got new aircraft and did a lot of training flying, both high and low level, finding it boring, and the crews, who were supposed to be the pick of Bomber Command, became "browned off." Men of other squadrons who were doing several ops. a week took to ragging them as the "One op. squadron".

Cochrane told Gibson he had done enough operations and would not let him fly again. Squadron Leader George Holden, D.S.O., D.F.C., arrived to take over, but Gibson stayed on for a few days. Holden was slight and youthful with fair wavy hair but a brusque manner. Before the war he had worn a bowler and carried a rolled umbrella, but was a very tough young man. He had felt very sick once but kept flying on ops. for over a week till he nearly collapsed after landing one night and went to the doctor, who examined him and said, a little startled, "Well, I think you've had pleurisy, but you seem to be nearly all right now."

617 went to war again on July 15, against power stations in Northern Italy. It was a long way, the aircraft would arrive with tanks two-thirds empty and there was no hope of flying back to England. Yells of joy when they were told they would fly on to Blida, an airfield in North Africa, near Algiers. The only glum one was Gibson, categorically forbidden to go.

It was a "cissy" trip; no opposition on the way, but they found the targets cloaked in haze and bombed largely by guess-work. Several aircraft were hit and Allsebrook lost an engine, but they all landed safely at Blida. At the de-briefing Mc-

Carthy threw his parachute down disgustedly and said, "You know, if we'd only carried flares tonight we could've seen what we were doing." No one took much notice just then, but it was that remark, remembered later, that was partly responsible for the history they made.

On the flight home they called at Leghorn to deliver some bombs over the docks, but again there was haze and they were not pleased with the bombing.

Martin flew back over the Alps at 19,000 feet, to the dismay of Tammy Simpson in the rear turret, who had thought they were returning low over France and had worn only his light tropical kit. Back at Scampton they thawed him out with rum.

Gibson was not there to meet them. He had gone. Harris and Cochrane had put a definite stop to his flying by asking Winston Churchill to take him with him to America for a "show the flag" tour, and Gibson had had no option. He'd been so upset he had not been able to face the farewells.

In August they were back to boredom. No ops., but training all and every day.

It was about this time that disturbing reports were coming out of Germany about a mysterious new weapon. Apparently Hitler's notorious "secret weapon". Agents could not say what it was but sensed it was something special. A couple of escaped prisoners of war reached England with information that hinted at rockets and indicated an area north-east of Luebeck. In the Pas de Calais area thousands of workmen were swarming about monstrous new concrete works. A recce aircraft brought back a photograph of a strange new factory at Peenemunde, north-east of Luebeck. Lying on the ground were pencil-shaped objects that baffled the interpretive men, but little by little they began to connect the rocket reports with the pencil-shaped objects and the concrete structures, which would obviously be impervious to any R.A.F. bombs. The 12,000-pounder thin-case bomb was nearly ready, but it was purely a blast bomb, to explode on the ground and knock over buildings. It would not dent masses of concrete half embedded in earth.

The spies were right. Seventy miles from London, just behind Calais, Hitler was building his secret-weapon blockhouses, fantastic structures which would bombard London and the invasion ports non-stop in spite of anything we could do. They were all of reinforced concrete, walls 16 feet thick and roofs 20 feet thick! No known bomb would affect them. The Todt Organisation promised Hitler that.

At Watton, Wizernes and Siracourt the blockhouses were to be assembly, storage and launching sites for rockets and flying bombs. Twelve thousand slaves were working on them, and deep under the concrete they were carving tunnels and chambers in the chalk and rock where Germans could live and fire their rockets without interruption.

But the greatest nightmare of all was the grotesque underworld being burrowed under a 20-foot thick slab of ferro-concrete near Mimoyecques. Here Hitler was preparing his V.3. Little has ever been told about V.3, probably because we never found out much about it. V.3 was the most secret and sinister of all—long-range guns with barrels 500 feet long!

The muzzles would never appear above earth; the entire barrels would be sunk in shafts that dived at 50 degrees 500 feet into the ground. Hitler was putting fifteen of these guns in at Mimoyecques, five guns, side by side, in each of three shafts. They were smooth-bore barrels, and a huge slow-burning charge would fire a 10-inch shell with a long, steady acceleration, so there would be no destructive heat and pressure in the barrel. In that way the barrels would not quickly wear out as Big Bertha did in World War I. These were more monstrous in every way than Big Bertha; they fired a bigger shell, could go on firing for a long time and, more important than that, they had a rapid rate of fire. Thick armour-plate doors in the concrete would slide back when they were ready, and then the nest of nightmare guns would pour out six shells a minute on London, 600 tons of explosives a day.

They would keep that up accurately day after day, so that in a fortnight London would receive as much high explosive as Berlin received during the whole war. But that fortnight would be only the start of it.

The War Cabinet did not know this, but they *did* know enough to be extremely worried. There were anxious (and very secret) conferences (which coincided with the fact that Cochrane was strongly pressing for renewed interest in Wallis's shock-wave bomb—he wanted to use it on the Rothensee ship-lift). Soon the Chief Executive of the Ministry of Aircraft Production, Air Chief Marshal Sir Wilfred Freeman, sent for Barnes Wallis, who was now held in esteem and some awe. Freeman said:

"Wallis, do you remember that crazy idea of yours back in 1940 about a bomb?"

"I seem to have had a lot of crazy ideas then," Wallis said wryly.

"I mean about a *big* bomb, a ten-tonner and a six-tonner. You wrote a paper about it. To penetrate deep into the earth and cause an earthquake."

"Ah, yes," said Wallis, his eyes lighting up.

"How soon can you let me have some?"

It was so sudden that Wallis was staggered. He thought a while.

"About four or five months," and he added quickly, "that is, if I get facilities. There's a lot of work to it, you know."

"Right. Will you go and see Craven right away, please. I'll ring him and tell him you're coming over."

Sir Charles Craven, head of Vickers, was also a Controller of the Ministry of Aircraft Production. Wallis was shown into his office near Whitehall ten minutes later, and before he could say a word Craven was booming at him:

"What d'you want the services of twenty thousand men in Sheffield for?" Apparently Freeman had already been on the phone.

Wallis explained and got a promise of full support. He had little time to relax in the next few weeks. First he held a "Dutch auction" with Roy Chadwick the Avro designer.

"Roy," he said, "can your Lancs carry seventeen thousand pounds for two hundred and fifty miles?"

"Oh yes," Chadwick said. "Easily."

"Could they carry nineteen thousand?"

"Oh . . . er . . . I think so."

"Well now, Roy," Wallis said persuasively, "how about going to the full ten tons?"

"Oh, I don't know about that."

"Now come on . . . if you tried more powerful engines and strengthened the undercarts."

"Well . . . Oh, I suppose it *could* be done."

"Thanks," said Wallis and went off to Sheffield to iron out more of the problems that seemed endless. The bomb had to be made from a *very* special steel; there were only two foundries in the country capable of casting the casings, and both were fully occupied on other vital work.

On August 30, 617 Squadron moved to Coningsby, another bomber airfield in Lincolnshire. Scampton had been a grass field, but Coningsby had long bitumen runways, more suitable for aircraft carrying very heavy loads. Flying was still confined to training, high and low level, aimlessly it seemed, and suddenly they were switched to low level. Cochrane told Holden that they had to be as good as they had been for the dams raid, and there were some new crews to train.

Cochrane and Satterly had long conferences with Holden and Group Captain Sam Patch, the station commander at Coningsby. There was a new verve about the squadron, a feeling of expectancy. At nights the aircraft hurtled low over the flat country and heavy lorries drove in to the bomb dump, their loads hidden under heavy tarpaulins. But it was not to be quite like the dams raid: that was obvious because they were still using the orthodox Lancasters. A flight of Mosquito night fighters arrived at Coningsby, and stayed. Apparently they were going to have fighter escort.

On September 14, Holden drew up a battle order for that night; a short one, eight crews, the pilots being Holden, Maltby, Knight, Shannon, Wilson, Allsebrook, Rice and Divall. Target was the Dortmund Ems Canal, the freight link between the Ruhr and central and eastern Germany, including the North Sea.

It was to be another very low-level raid, partly for bombing accuracy and partly because they thought the flak low down was less of a risk than fighters high up, concentrating on eight lonely aircraft. Cochrane saw that it was one of the most carefully planned raids of the war. As in the dams raid, the route curled delicately between the known flak. A specially designed beacon would be dropped near the canal as a pin-point and night fighters would engage the flak which guarded the most vulnerable points on the canal, although not the point chosen for the attack, which was some two miles from the nearest guns. A weather recce plane would check the visibility in the canal area before the Lancasters arrived. Most important of all they were going to drop the new 12,000-lb. light-case bombs for the first time. (Not to be confused with Wallis's developing earthquake bomb.)

They took off at dusk with no illusions; memories of the dams losses were too fresh and they had a human yearning for the placid if less stimulating days of the Italian trips.

They were an hour out, low over the North Sea, when the weather Mosquito found the target hidden under fog and radioed back. Group recalled the Lancasters and as the big aircraft turned for home weighed down by nearly 6 tons of bomb David Maltby seemed to hit someone's slipstream; a wing flicked down, the nose dipped and before Maltby could correct it the wing-tip had caught the water and the Lancaster cartwheeled, dug her nose in and vanished in spray. Shannon swung out of formation and circled the spot, sending out radio fixes and staying till an air sea rescue flying boat touched down beneath. They waited up at Coningsby till the flying boat radioed that it had found nothing but oil slicks.

Maltby's wife lived near the airfield, and in the morning Holden went over to break the news, dreading it because it had been an ideally happy marriage. Maltby was only twenty-one. The girl met him at the door and guessed his news from his face.

"It was quick," said Holden, who did not know it was his own last day on earth. "He wouldn't have known a thing."

Too stunned to cry, the girl said, "I think we both expected it. He's been waking up in the night lately shouting something about the bomb not coming off."

Holden came back looking tired and got out another battle order. If the weather was right the raid was on again. Martin came back from leave that morning and demanded to take Maltby's place. Tammy Simpson, who had been flying with Martin for two years now, noted philosophically and a little querulously in his diary: "Mick's a fool volunteering. This is going to be dangerous." Shannon was hoping the weather would be right this time. Moustacheless, he was to marry Anne in a week and was supposed to have left for London that morning to arrange the wedding. Anne had already wangled a posting for herself to Dunholme Lodge, an airfield near Coningsby.

At dusk in the control tower McCarthy watched the heavy aircraft lift off the runway and head east. Over the North Sea the Lancasters kept loose formation in two boxes of four. It felt like the dams raid all over again; they were down to 50 feet to fox the radar and on strict radio silence. The faster Mosquitoes would be taking off now to pass them somewhere on the way in and set about the flak as the bombers arrived. Over the canal itself the weather Mosquito radioed back that it was perfectly clear.

The bombers crossed the Dutch coast and there was no sign of flak. Holden seemed to be flying a perfect course, which was just as well because the moon was up and it was full, throwing soft light over the fields as they moved towards Germany and Ladbergen.

Ahead of them a small town loomed up and high chimneys and a church steeple seemed to be rushing at them. Martin waited for Holden to swing to one side, but Holden elected to bore straight across and climbed to clear the steeple till he was about 300 feet. The more low-flying-wise Martin dropped right down to roof-top height and, on the other side of Holden, Knight and Wilson did the same, till even from the ground they were nearly invisible against the horizon. Holden was limned against the moonlight.

There was one light gun in Nordhoorn and its crew had been alerted. Holden was half-way across when a procession of glowing red balls streamed up, and in a shaven fraction of a second Toby Foxlee was firing back, so that only about five shells pumped up before Foxlee's tracer was squirting down and the gun promptly stopped.

One of the five shells punched into Holden's inner starboard wing tank. There was a long streamer of flame trailing back beyond the tailplane; the aircraft showed clearly in the glow and they could see it was going down. The port wing was dropping and then the nose; she was falling faster, slewing to the left, right under Wilson and Knight with a 12,000-pounder on board! Martin yelled sharply over the R/T: "Break outwards!"

Wilson was just turning away when Holden's aircraft hit on the edge of the town almost under him; the 12,000-pounder went off and the town and the sky were like day.

Martin called the other two anxiously. Knight came right back and said he was all right, but it was twenty seconds before Wilson answered, a little shakily, saying they were jarred by the explosion but he thought nothing serious was broken. A little later they were back in formation, Martin leading. They swept into Germany, grimmer now. Gibson's crew had been in Holden's aircraft. Spafford, Taerum, Pulford, Hutchinson; they were all gone.

One by one they picked up pin-points and the canal was only five minutes away when a blanket seemed to come down in front and they found themselves in mist. It was unbelievable. The area had been clear and moonlit half an hour before, no trace of trouble, and now the ground was a smudge, and they edged up to over a hundred feet to be clear of obstacles. The fog had moved in from the east without warning, almost without precedent.

There were locks along the canal and every one was armed with flak. The trouble was that the Lancasters could not see the canal until they were right on it, and then it was too late to bomb. They would have to bomb from 150 feet—because they could not see the canal if they went any higher—and hope the flak would miss, which at that height was unlikely.

All of them tried flying across the canal to pick it up, hoping they could swing sharply on to it, but found it was nearly impossible. Split up now, they searched the area but kept blundering into the flak, and then they turned away and tried again, refusing to bomb till they were certain they were in position. The Mosquitoes had arrived and, with their greater speed and smaller size, were charging back and forth trying to silence the gunners, but could not pick them up in the fog.

Allsebrook is believed to have bombed eventually but where his bomb went is not known. They never found the wreckage of his aircraft either. Wilson was heard briefly over the R/T saying something about going in to attack. The bomb was still aboard when the aircraft hit the ground about 200 yards beyond the canal and made a crater 200 feet across. Divall was heard briefly over the R/T, but that was the last anyone ever heard from him.

The gentle little Les Knight shouted over the intercom. that he could see the water, and then flak was coming at them and they were weaving. Johnson, the bomb aimer, yelled that he could see trees looming ahead and *above* them, and as Knight pulled up hard the bomber shuddered as she hit the tree-tops, and then they were clear with branches stuffed in the radiators, both port engines stopped and the tailplane damaged.

With the two starboard engines roaring at full power the Lancaster, with the bomb still aboard, was able to hold her height. No chance of bombing in that condition, and Knight called up Martin: "Two port engines gone. May I have permission to jettison bomb, sir?" It was the "sir" that got Martin. Quiet little Knight was following the copybook procedure, asking respectful permission to do the only thing that might get him home.

Martin said, "For God's sake, Les, yes," and as the bomb was not fused Knight told Johnson to let it go. Relieved of the weight they started to climb very slowly.

After the gunners had thrown out all the guns and fittings they could, Knight got her up to about 1,400 feet and headed towards England, the aircraft waffling soggily at 110 m.p.h. The controls were getting worse all the time until, though he had full opposite rudder and aileron on, Knight could not stop her turning to port and it was obvious he could never fly her home. He ordered his crew to bale out and held the plane steady while they did. When the last man had gone he must have tried to do the same himself, and must have known all the time what would happen when he slipped out of his seat. There was perhaps a slight chance of getting clear in time, but as soon as he took pressure off stick and rudder the aircraft flicked on her back and plunged to the ground. Knight did not get to the hatch in time.

Geoff Rice tried for an hour to find the canal, was badly holed by flak and finally had to swing his winged aircraft out of the area, jettison the bomb and head for home. Shannon was seventy minutes before he got a quick sight of the high banks of the canal, wheeled the Lancaster along the water and Sumpter called, "Bomb gone!" There was an eleven-second delay on the fuse, so they only dimly saw the explosion. The bomb hit the tow-path. If it had been a few feet to one side, in the water, it would have breached the canal wall.

Martin spent an hour and a half plunging at 150 feet in the fog around the canal trying to give Bob Hay a good enough sight on the few spots where the high earth bank was vulnerable. Now and then he caught a brief glimpse of the water, but it was either at a spot where the banks were low and solid or the flak was too murderous to give them a chance. It squirted at them when they were right on top of it and they had to wheel away into the fog. The aircraft jolted twice as shells punched into it, and once a sudden burst of tracer ripped through under the cockpit so that Martin jumped with shock, one foot slipped off the rudder bar and the big Lancaster swung so crazily he thought it was all over.

The gunners had been firing whenever they got a chance and Tammy Simpson reported his ammunition was getting low. Martin told him to forget the flak and save what he had left in case they got a chance to fight their way home.

Once or twice he was able to come up to the canal diagonally so that it was easier to turn along it, but each time the glimpse of water came too late or the flak was coming point blank at them and they had to pull away.

On the thirteenth run Hay got a glimpse of water in the swirling fog and called, "There it is!" Martin turned away in a slow and regular 360 degrees circle, opening his bomb doors and calculating the exact moment he should come over the water again so the straighten-up would be gentle. It was a beautifully timed turn; they were low over the sliver of water with no flak, just long enough for Hay to call, "Left, left, a shade right . . . bomb gone!" and then Whittaker slammed the throttles hard on and Martin pulled her steeply round as the flak opened up.

A little later they hurtled back across the canal and saw the water boiling where the bomb had exploded, a few feet from the bank, just a few feet too far, because the bank was still there.

They were still over Germany and dawn was breaking as they came out of the fog. On full throttle, "P Popsie" was shaking at 267 m.p.h., the fastest she had ever travelled at low level. As they slid round the end of Sylt two last guns sent shells after them and then they were over the sea.

They landed two hours overdue and found Cochrane still waiting. He had heard of the losses from Shannon, who was first back, and his face was leaner and grimmer than ever. Martin was the third back, out of eight. Cochrane knew there would not be any more. He said:

"How was it?"

"I'm terribly sorry, sir," Martin said. "It didn't breach. The mist beat us, and the flak." He told what had happened. Cochrane listened keenly and at the end he was staggered when Martin said, "I'm very disappointed, sir, but if the weather's clear tomorrow—I mean, that is, tonight now—I think we can get it, if you'll let us have another crack."

"How many crews have you got left?"

Martin thought for a while and said, "Well, there are three of us in my flight, and three more in Shannon's flight. That ought to be enough, sir."

"Six!" Cochrane said. "Out of your original twenty-one!"

"It ought to be enough, sir. I'm just sorry about last night."

Cochrane said gently, "I don't think you have to apologise for anything, Martin. I'll let you know later about tonight. Meantime you'd better go and get some sleep." He took Sam Patch by the arm and led him over to the corner and Patch for the first time sensed that Cochrane had let slip the mask of his reserve. There was no mistaking it, and almost no defining it, an intensity about his eyes, his whole face and his voice as he said:

"Patch, I'd like to make Martin a wing commander on the spot and put him in command of the squadron. You know the boy better than I do. Would you recommend him?"

Patch thought for a moment before he made the answer for which he has been kicking himself ever since: "It's two jumps up the ladder, sir; I'm not sure he's ready for it. He's had no experience in administration."

"Well, I'll at least get him made a squadron leader and give him temporary command." Cochrane caught Martin as he finished stowing his kit away and said in his sudden-death way, "You're a squadron leader now, Martin, and for the time being you're in command of the squadron."

Martin looked after the retreating back. A moment before he hadn't even been a flight commander. Patch said, "Well, you've got responsibilities now, Mick. Come and have a walk and talk till you relax." Martin was too exhilarated to sleep. They paced slowly across the airfield, right to the blast walls of the bomb dump, lonely in its isolation on the far side of the field.

"I didn't think anything could have gone wrong," Patch was saying. "I thought we had the perfect plan this time."

"Oh, we should've pranged the thing," Martin said disgustedly. "That mist. You couldn't see a thing."

There was a long silence; the air was fresh, the grass soft and springy under their feet, and Martin, after eight hours in the air, was far from sleep with the light-headed exhilaration you get after you're so tired you can hardly stand and then get your second wind. He had been awake over twenty-four hours. He said suddenly: "Well, there it is, sir. Two real ops, and six crews left. Maybe this is the end. They'll make us an ordinary line squadron . . . or disband us altogether."

"Probably *will* be the end if you try that canal again tonight," Patch said dryly. "You were silly to volunteer again. You're not immortal."

"No, sir."

"D'you think you'd get away with it again tonight?"

"Couldn't be any worse."

"I suppose it occurs to you the flak will be expecting you."

Martin said soberly, "I suppose so."

"Forget it a while, Mick," Patch said. "I don't think the A.O.C.'ll let you try again for a while anyway. He doesn't like losing crews, and you lost five out of eight last night . . . six including Maltby the night before. You'll lose the rest if you go again tonight. We've got to think out a cleverer way of doing it."

There was another silence and Patch broke it by saying tentatively:

"What d'you think about 617 taking a rest for a while? You've taken an awful beating and you've got to fill up with new crews and train them. What d'you think?"

Martin said, "No. Let's do another one right away and get the taste out of our mouths. Otherwise we're going to get scared of going back."

"The A.O.C.'ll decide that anyway," Patch said. "Maybe you've had your day on special duty."

They called at the office on the way back to see about the casualty reports, but Chiefy Powell was already attending to them. Patch took Martin over to the mess for breakfast and sat and talked to him. Patch had not been to sleep for nearly thirty hours himself but he never changed his routine when a raid was on. He never failed to visit every aircraft before it took off; always waited up till the last crew had landed and then went over to the mess with them for bacon and eggs and yarned as long as they wanted him to. He never went to bed himself till he'd seen the last of the boys off to bed. He was a round-faced, heavy-set, youngish man, direct and honest. If you did a good job, Patch would go to tremendous trouble to let you know. If you did a bad job he would tell you how and why, so you would do better next time. If you failed to mend your ways he would crack down hard, and then in the mess that night he would be normal and friendly to the punished one.

As Martin was finishing breakfast McCarthy and the laconic Munro came in, clicked their heels and peeled off sizzling salutes. "Good morning, *sir*," they chorused, and Martin had the grace to blush. They congratulated him and, in grimmer mood, paid their respects to the dead. Martin gave his first orders. "Will you get cracking on making what aircraft we've got left ready for tonight. I'm thinking we'll be on again. Let me know when the target comes through." He added, almost as an after-thought, "May be the same target tonight."

"All right," said McCarthy. "Push off to bed and grab some shuteye."

Shannon had only got to bed himself about half an hour before. He had written a little note to Anne, apologising for not being able to go up to London. Anne got it over at Dunholme Lodge that afternoon. Quite a short note: "Sorry, darling. Couldn't make it. Been up two nights. Lost six out of nine. Please forgive. I'm rather tired." For the first time she saw the writing was shaky.

She had been up all night herself in the ops. room at Dunholme Lodge. About dawn they got a report that five out of the eight were shot down and she was crying when someone ran over and said, "David's all right. He's back." But the tears only fell faster.

Martin got nearly five hours sleep. McCarthy regretfully woke him at two o'clock, shaking his shoulder and saying, "Target's through, Mick," until the tired boy shook the sleep out of his head and said, "Where?"

"Somewhere in the south of France. Bridge or something."

Martin pulled some clothes on and saw Patch over in the planning room. Patch said, "You're not going back to the canal yet. You're going with 619 Squadron to have a go at the Antheor Viaduct. It's on the Riviera, near the Eytie border, and carries the only good railway into Italy from France. If you prang it you'll stop half the Hun reinforcements to Sicily."

Martin said, "I'm sorry it isn't the canal," and he so obviously meant it that Patch just looked at him.

They found the viaduct without trouble fifteen miles west of Cannes, seeing in the moonlight the 90-foot stone arches curving across the beach at the foot of a ravine. The idea was to dive to 300 feet and stab 1,000-lb. bombs into the stone with delayed fuses. It was like a coco-nut shy; bang on and the coco-nut is yours, miss by an inch and lose your money. They missed by inches. The bombs went through the arches and exploded on the ground all around; the viaduct was pitted by splinters but that was all. The only real result was that it woke the Germans up to the vulnerability of the railway, and soon after that the flak batteries moved in.

Shannon scrounged a few days' leave, went up to London and married Anne. They spent part of their honeymoon in a hotel, and when they walked into the bar one night Anne heard someone say, "That boy looks too young to be in the Air Force." Shannon turned round and the man saw he was wearing a D.S.O. and D.F.C. and his eyes stuck out like organ stops.

Cochrane sent for Martin. "I think we might be able to use this dams bomb of Wallis's against the *Tirpitz*," the A.O.C. said. The *Tirpitz* was still sheltering in Alten Fiord. "You can't fly up the fiord to get her; that'd be death, but she's moored only about half a mile from the shore where the land rises steeply. You might do it by surprise, hurdle the hill, dive and bomb before they wake up." There was a hill near Bangor, he said, about the same height and gradient. Martin was to go and practise over it to see if he could level out soon enough on the water at the right height and speed.

Martin flew "P Popsie" over to North Wales and spent an afternoon diving over the coast, climbing and trying again. It called for most delicate judgment, but towards the end he found he could do it with 40 degrees of flap down. It meant diving 60 m.p.h. faster than permitted with 40 degrees of flap and that meant the flap was likely to collapse on one side. If that happened at low level the aircraft would spin straight in. He reported to Cochrane that he was willing to chance that. He knew what the *Tirpitz* defences would be like at low level but thought the raid would be possible.

"We wouldn't need too many aircraft, sir. Myself, McCarthy and Shannon would go. I don't imagine there will be much chance of a second run, but we know the form of attack well and we could practise over the Bangor hills so we get it right the first time." He suggested they do the raid by moon-light or at dusk or dawn, so there would be some gloom for cover but enough light to see the ship. Matter-of-factly he added: "I think you should be prepared to lose the three air-craft, sir, but we'll have a go and probably get her."

Cochrane, who had not met anyone quite like Martin before, looked at him for some time and finally said, "Well, I'll let you know about it. Meantime start building up the squadron again with new crews. I'll have some picked ones sent to you."

(Actually it was not the *Tirpitz* that Cochrane was after at this time. "Tirpitz" was the "cover plan" to camouflage the real plan. He was, in fact, scheming to smash the big dam at Modane, in Italy, and the hills around Bangor resembled the hill around Modane Dam. Martin discovered that seven years later.)

Martin was interviewing new pilots and crews for the next week, and it was not easy. 617's fame—or notoriety—had spread and it was known as a suicide squadron. Some quite brave men were posted to it but told Martin openly they did not want to stay. Martin did not argue. They were quite willing to fly with their own squadrons, where perhaps one crew in ten finished a tour; in 617 it seemed that no crew had a chance. He did not press anyone who was not willing—they would be no good to him—but sent them back to their old squadrons, and after a week had found only four crews willing to join him: O'Shaughnessy, Willsher, Weedon and Bull. He was doubtful about accepting Willsher because Willsher looked younger even than Shannon, only nineteen, a thin, fair boy a year out of school.

Willsher had trouble finding a crew until a red-faced broken-nosed, tough-looking Londoner called Gerry Witherick in-sisted on being his rear gunner. Witherick was unkillable. He had flown nearly a hundred missions and was a hard case with a soft heart and a riotous wit.

CHAPTER X

SNIPER SQUADRON

THE fate of 617 was decided at high level. "We'll make 'em a special duties squadron," said Sir Arthur Harris. "They needn't do ordinary ops., but whenever the Army or Navy want a dam or a ship or something clouted we'll put 617 on to it. And we'll put all the old lags in 617."

"The old lags" was Harris's affectionate and respectful name for the really hard-bitten aircrews who only wanted to do operations. Every now and then there would be a crew who, after finishing their tour, would stubbornly boggle at taking their six months' rest training new aircrews. They insisted on staying on operations and were dearest of all to Harris, probably because they had the same volcanic temperament as himself.

Harris said 617 could stay in 5 Group with Cochrane, and Cochrane had it in his mind to make them a "sniper" squadron for super-accurate bombing with Wallis's 10-tonner. Ordinary bombing, he knew, would waste most of the 10-tonners, and there would be none to waste.

Up to this time a little more than one out of three raids were really effective. The Germans built dummy targets outside cities, spread camouflage nets over tell-tale lakes and rivers in the towns, decoyed the bombers in every way they could, and even lit fires in fields so the bombers would think they were hitting their targets. Often the crews bombed open fields instead.

That was why the Pathfinder Force had been formed, and now that they were in action bombing was becoming more effective. P.F.F. found and marked the target areas with coloured flares, and the main force bombed these markers. It stopped them bombing open fields, but it was still "carpet bombing", hateful, and yet, it seemed, necessary.

And losses still mounted. Now they were about 4 per cent; one bomber in twenty-five failed to return. Or average it another way—a squadron of twenty aircraft would lose every one in twenty-five raids. A tour of operation was thirty raids; then, if you were still alive, you had six months' rest and went back for another tour. In lives and labour and for the minor damage done, bombing was not economical enough for Harris.

At Farnborough, in 1941, a man named Richards had invented a piece of intricate mechanism he called the Stabilising Automatic Bomb Sight. It incorporated a gyro; in perfect conditions it could aim a bomb uncannily, but Harris thought it was too complicated for the conditions of actual bombing. For one thing, a bomber using it had to run perfectly straight and level up to the target for ten miles, a perfect mark for flak, searchlights and fighters. Harris said it would mean death for too many of his boys, who had little enough chance as it was, and Bomber Command could not take much heavier losses.

Another school of thought said the S.A.B.S. *could* be used economically by a small force. Cochrane was one of them. He argued that from high level the S.A.B.S. could hit a well-marked target so accurately that they would not have to send the squadrons back to the same place again and again. In the long run they would lose less. He wanted to train 617 till they could use the S.A.B.S. in battle and deliver Wallis's 10-tonners, when they arrived, in the right spots.

There were many conferences and then Harris agreed.

Patch called Martin to his office. "The *Tirpitz* is off for the time being," he said, and Martin sighed gently with relief. "The A.O.C. has something new for you. From now on your squadron role is changed to ultra-accurate high-level bombing and you're going to be practising till your eyes drop out.

You've got to get down to an *average* of *under* a hundred yards from twenty thousand feet." Martin's eyes almost dropped out on the spot. "The reasons," Patch went on, "are that there's a new bomb coming up . . . a big one. You'll only be able to carry one and they're so expensive every one will have to be spot on." He said they were getting a new bomb sight at once.

A day later a tall, thin man with lively eyes walked into Martin's office carrying a bundle wrapped in oilskin and announced that he was Squadron Leader Richardson come to help 617 convert to the S.A.B.S.

"This is it," he said, carefully unwrapping the bundle. "It's the loveliest thing in the world." The S.A.B.S. looked like an ordinary bomb sight except that a bulky gyro was encased in it. Richardson handled it lovingly, and in the next few days the squadron found out why. He was not a bomb-aiming enthusiast, he was a fanatic who started talking bomb-aiming at breakfast and was still on the subject at bedtime. He lectured the crews, flew with them, experimented with them and after a time no one had any chance of not knowing everything about the S.A.B.S. Bob Hay, haunted now by his own profession, christened him "Talking Bomb". Much of the credit for what happened belongs to "Talking Bomb", who had been a pilot in World War I and managed in due course to fly on fifteen raids with 617 to watch his beloved bomb sight in action.

617 did no ops. for weeks, but night and day the aircraft were 20,000 feet over the bombing range at Wainfleet aiming practice bombs at the white dots on the sands with the S.A.B.S. It needed far more than a hawk-eyed bomb aimer; it called for teamwork. The gunners took drifts to help the navigator work out precise wind direction and speed, and navigator and bomb aimer calculated obscure instrument corrections. An error of a few feet at 20,000 feet would throw a bomb hopelessly off.

"Talking Bomb" himself was very accurate with the S.A.B.S., and before long a couple of crews could emulate him. Martin's was one. Within three weeks Hay set an example with an average of 64 yards. Some of the others, however, were still well over a hundred yards.

Three more crews arrived: Bill Suggitt, Canadian squadron leader, to take over A Flight, Clayton and Ted Youseman, an Englishman, who never stopped talking flying. There were the usual incidents—two aircraft hit trees low flying and were written off (though no one was killed). Martin had an engine catch fire in the air but doused it with the extinguishers. Shannon's aileron cables snapped over the North Sea, but he made an emergency landing, using trimmers to keep his wing-tips level and making a wide, flat turn on rudder alone. He claimed it was better than his usual landing, which, Sumpter said rudely, was nothing to boast about.

Spurred on by Cochrane, Sam Patch and Martin tried to find a way of minimising the danger of the ten-mile run-up to the target using S.A.B.S. "Talking Bomb" was a fertile source of ideas.

"This is what you ought to do," he said. "You all fly round the target in a great big circle like Red Indians, see? and then someone gives the word and you all turn inwards and come in like the spokes of a wheel. The Hun won't know who to shoot at."

"That's O.K., Talking Bomb," Martin said, "but what happens when they all get into the middle?"

"Oh, put 'em at different heights."

"What about the bombs falling on the lower aircraft?"

"There must be a way over that," "Talking Bomb" muttered.

It was a somewhat similar idea that they adopted, and it depended on immaculate timing and navigation. The aircraft, at different heights, would circle a spot in sight of the target but outside the defences, and when the markers were down the leader would assess their accuracy, give the order to bomb and they would all come in, converging slightly. If there were twenty guns below, for instance, and only one aircraft coming in, the twenty guns would all be firing at it, but with twenty planes coming in at the same time, too widely scattered for a box barrage, there would be only one gun against each aircraft—twenty times less chance of being hit.

New troubles kept cropping up with the S.A.B.S. For instance, the thermometers were showing errors up to 5 degrees, enough to throw a bomb over a hundred feet the wrong way. Farnborough put in new type thermometers, and by early November the squadron had an average bombing error of only 90 yards.

Good enough, Cochrane thought, and at dusk on November 12, Martin led the squadron off to try out the S.A.B.S. in battle. The target was the Antheor Viaduct again, an easy one so that they could give the S.A.B.S. fair trial. In the bomb bays hung 12,000-lb. light-case "blast" bombs.

They found the viaduct in half-moonlight, but this time it was different . . . four searchlights and half a dozen guns round it. Running up, the viaduct was hard to pick up in the glare of the searchlights; the next little bay looked exactly the same and several crews bombed the wrong bay. Some of them got the right bay in their graticules but could not distinguish the viaduct. Rice, O'Shaughnessy and one other got near misses, 50 yards away, but the blast was not enough to damage the viaduct.

They flew disgustedly on to Blida again and it was then that Martin recalled what McCarthy had said about flares after San Polo. Everyone agreed that if they had had flares to mark the viaduct they could have hit it. Two days later they flew back to England, but Youseman never arrived. No one ever found out what happened to him and his crew, but a German fighter probably got them over the sea.

Martin reported to Cochrane the need for target marking, and Cochrane sent him and Patch to Pathfinder Headquarters to talk it over with the experts. Pathfinders promised to mark their next target, and Martin put the crews back on training to perfect their S.A.B.S. technique.

Martin's time as temporary commander was up. Cochrane would not replace him with any ordinary squadron commander, but he had found the man he wanted. Leonard Cheshire, at twenty-five, was the youngest group captain in the R.A.F., and was not only willing to return to operations but actually asked Cochrane to drop him back to wing commander so he could take over the squadron. He did not look the part at all. Gibson had looked the part; but Cheshire looked more like a theological student thinly disguised as a senior officer; yet he had done two tours and won a D.S.O. and bar and D.F.C. He was tall, thin and dark, a strange blend of brilliance (sometimes erratic), self-consciousness, confidence and soft-spoken charm. Highly sensitive and introspective, he yet lacked, quite illogically, the foreboding imagination that makes some sensitive men sweat with fear before a raid.

He had a gentle consideration for other people, and a Puckish sense of humour, but in the air he was cool, efficient and calculating. In a way he had a mind like Barnes Wallis, liable to get ideas that horrified people but turned out to be right. He had been flying a certain type of heavy bomber at a time when losses of that type were inexplicably heavy. They had acquired too much extra equipment, so that fully loaded, at operational height, they were slow, flew soggily and were inclined to yaw and drop into a fatal spiral with the rudders locked over. Then they added kidney cowls to blanket the exhaust flames from night fighters, and that, for Cheshire, was the last straw. He considered it made the aircraft more dangerous than the enemy and asked permission to take the cowls off his squadron's aircraft.

Everyone flatly disagreed except his A.O.C., Air Vice-Marshal Carr, who let Cheshire do so, with the result that his losses fell. It was the first step to taking off a lot more: front turret, mid-upper turret and armour-plate; freed of the excessive drag and weight the plane flew more comfortably, the engines were not overworked and losses fell further.

* * *

A raid on Peenemunde had put Germany's rocket programme back six months, and they stopped work on the monster rocket blockhouses to go ahead with the more dispersed flying-bomb sites. Recce aircraft were bringing back to England photographs showing mysterious new activity in the same areas, the erection of many low, curved buildings in clearings in woods, and next to them short sets of rails that seemed to start and end in nothingness. Intelligence men christened them "ski sites" because the long buildings were the same shape as skis, and bit by bit they connected them more definitely with secret-weapon reports.

It was clear that these and other satellite launching sites could be put up very quickly and were more or less mobile. They were springing up all over the place and ordinary blast bombs could smash them, but after Peenemunde, Hitler seemed to be relying for protection on dispersal—numbers, camouflage and mobility—instead of three or four centralised targets.

In Whitehall, Churchill, the Air Council, Harris, Sir Stafford Cripps (now Minister of Aircraft Production) and Sir Wilfred Freeman discussed the situation uncomfortably, and one day Freeman sent for Wallis.

"We're stopping work on the ten-ton bomb," he said. "The big targets we had for them aren't so important now, and Sir Stafford doesn't think the ten-tonner justifies all that work."

Wallis could not dispute the logic of it. The biggest bombers would have a very short range with a ten-tonner—little more than across the Channel, and in that area there seemed no other targets important enough. There were plenty in Germany, of course, but the Lancasters could not carry the 10-tonner as far as that.

Wallis pleaded with Freeman to let him go ahead with the 12,000-lb. scaled-down version of the 10-tonner, to penetrate deeply in the same way and cause an earthquake shock. The Lancasters could drop them deep inside Germany on the kind of targets he had originally had in mind. Freeman thought for a long time, and in the end he said yes—a bold decision to make on his own. He knew that neither the Air Council nor the Ministry of Supply liked the idea of either the 10-tonner or the scaled-down version, because they were designed to be dropped from 40,000 feet for proper penetration. The Lancaster could not drop them from higher than 20,000, and the Council and Ministry considered they would not thus penetrate deeply enough for the proper earthquake effect.

Freeman made the decision so much on his own initiative that no Requirement Order was issued for the bombs, which meant that the Air Force did not have to accept them—or pay for them. He gave the scaled-down bomb the code name of "Tallboy", and Wallis hoped to have one ready for trial by March.

Cochrane had his eye on the mobile launching sites as targets for 617 but left them in peace while Cheshire kept his crews perfecting the S.A.B.S. technique, and for some weeks the squadron did no operations until, on December 10, Cheshire got a call from Tempsford for the loan of four crews. Tempsford was the hush-hush airfield where planes took off to land agents in occupied countries and drop arms to Resistance fighters. Cheshire chose McCarthy, Clayton, Bull and Weedon, and they flew their aircraft to Tempsford.

McCarthy landed back at Coningsby two days later, walked into Humphries' office and dumped two kitbags on the floor. "Bull and Weedon's kit," he said. "They've had it."

"Oh God! When?"

"Last night. We did a special low-level thing, dropping arms and ammunition. They must have hit trouble." He added disgustedly, "I didn't even find the target area."

He went back to Tempsford that afternoon, and he and Clayton tried again that night—successfully.

CHAPTER XI

DIRECT HIT

HARRIS had been sending bombers by day to smash at the mysterious "ski sites" in the Pas de Calais, but too many German fighters swarmed up to protect them. It left him with a pretty problem . . . the targets were so small and well hidden that the squadrons would not be able to pin-point and bomb them accurately by night. Cochrane asked permission for 617 to try their precision bombing with P.F.F. (Pathfinder Force) to mark the pin-points with incendiaries, and Harris agreed.

Night after night 617 was briefed, but the target was smothered under low stratus cloud until, on December 16, Cheshire led nine Lancasters off. A Pathfinder "oboe" Mosquito flew with them to mark the target. "Oboe" was a new way of radar pin-pointing; two beams went out from England and crossed exactly over the target to let the pilot know when he was there. This night the "oboe" plane dropped a casket of incendiaries, and they cascaded into the wood that hid the "ski site". At 10,000 feet 617 saw them winking among the trees like tiny glow-worms, swung in together according to the drill, nicely scattered so that the flak was ineffective, and all the 12,000-pounder "blast" bombs went down within a couple of minutes. Around the incendiaries the wood erupted in flame.

Back at Coningsby they developed the aiming-point photos (taken by photo-flash) and a groan went up. The markers had been 350 yards from the target; the bombs were all round the markers with an average error of only 94 yards, but that meant that the bombing was so good that the ski site was untouched.

It was the most accurate high-level night bombing of the war, but that made it all the more bitter.

It confirmed a suspicion both Cheshire and Cochrane had had . . . Pathfinders were fine for area marking but not precise enough for pin-point targets. Martin suggested they drop parachute flares over the target, lighting up the area so that a couple of aircraft could dive to low level and drop incendiary markers "spot on" the target. Cheshire agreed, but Cochrane, with the memory of the Dortmund Ems painfully fresh in his mind, would not hear of more low-level work.

Cheshire and Martin went off quietly and tried low-level marking on the ranges in the hope that they could get Cochrane to change his mind. They dropped practice bombs from about 200 feet using the low-level bomb sight and were only mildly satisfied with the results. They found they could land a bomb accurately but the trajectory was so flat that the bomb tended to bounce and skid 200 yards beyond the target. And at night-time they found in the Lancasters that they were shooting past the range target before they saw it.

On December 20 they tried P.F.F. "oboe" marking again on an armament factory near Liege but found the town hopelessly cloaked under low cloud. On the way back (with their bombs) Martin saw a Lancaster going down in flames with one of the gunners still firing at the fighter. Back at Coningsby they waited up, more out of conscience than hope, but Geoff Rice one of the five survivors of the original squadron, did not return.

The weather closed in until the night of December 30, when they went with an "oboe" plane to another ski site. Three bombs were direct hits on the "oboe" markers, but the markers were again a couple of hundred yards off the target and the ski site escaped.

Chesire pleaded with Cochrane for permission to mark at low level. His idea was that P.F.F. should drop flares by "oboe" to illuminate the area, and he and Martin should fly low enough to put a marker right on the spot.

Cochrane replied with a flat "No", and added, "Try and find another way. Try marking with the S.A.B.S. from about five thousand feet. If you can light the area enough with flares to get a sight, you ought to be able to do it accurately."

Cheshire suggested in that case that 617 might as well carry their own flares and dispense with the Pathfinders. Cochrane agreed and on January 4 they flew back to the Pas de Calais without the "oboe" plane. From 12,000 feet the squadron dropped floating flares, but cloud foiled Cheshire and Martin at 5,000 feet, so they both dived to 400 feet (pre-arranged and strictly off the record) and skimmed over the dim clearing from different directions. The markers landed in the clearing but both sets bounced and skidded 100 yards into the woods, so that the clearing was straddled by them.

The squadron managed to put most of their bombs between the markers, badly damaging the ski site; Cheshire thought it was fairly successful but was not exactly delighted . . . skidding markers were too uncertain to rely on. In the next few days he, Martin and "Talking Bomb" kept experimenting to find a permissible way of marking.

Between 3,000 and 6,000 feet on a clear aiming point by day they found they could put down a marker within 40 yards of a target—near enough for Cochrane—but could not do it on a hazy target, and there was little chance of getting a clear enough aiming point at night. Moonlight and flares would help, but any important target was going to be camouflaged.

That was the week the squadron moved from Coningsby to Woodhall Spa, about ten miles away. Woodhall was a one-squadron station and that was the reason for the move. As a "special duties" squadron on new and rather hush-hush projects, Cochrane wanted them to go on working in somewhat exclusive isolation.

Cheshire and Martin kept experimenting to find a way of marking, and one day, flying back from the range, Martin saw a patch of seaweed in the water that took his fancy. Always ready to spice his flying with a little variety he peeled off in one of his usual spectacular turns, dived steeply and dropped a bomb. It was a direct hit.

When he landed he jumped out of "P Popsie" quivering with excitement. "That's it, sir," he said jauntily to Cheshire. "We've got it. I didn't use the bomb-sight when I dropped that thing over the seaweed and it was a piece of cake. If we can dive-bomb markers point-blank over a target we can put 'em right on the button without the bomb sight and they won't skid off. What's more, we could see the target much better from above than coming up to it down low."

Cheshire went out and tried it that afternoon and it worked like a charm, almost without practice.

Next night they went back to the Pas de Calais. Munro dropped flares and Martin, turning a blandly blind eye to orders, tried his new method, peeling off, sticking his nose steeply down and aiming his whole aircraft at the ski site. He found that dive-bombing low at night in a four-engined plane was a slightly hair-raising business but dropped his markers in the dive and pulled out at about 400 feet. They were a new type of marker, red and green flares known as "spot fires", and as he pulled up and levelled off Martin saw the two lights like red and green eyes winking in the middle of the clearing. It was a clear night; from 12,000 feet they were plainly visible, and the rest of the squadron plastered the rocket site out of existence.

A couple of nights later they went to another flying-bomb site; Martin dived low again, laid his spot fires accurately and a few minutes later the target was littered about a few smoking craters.

Cheshire went to Cochrane and told him of the new method (that is, told him of the seaweed and the trials over the range, not of Martin's actual dives over the targets). Knowing that Cochrane approved of low-level marking on every count except the risk, Cheshire assured him that the diving attack, straight down, up and away, with only a few fleeting seconds near the ground, was reasonably safe. He added earnestly:

"Sir, if we're going to mark accurately we *must* be low enough to see exactly what we're doing, and I'm sure that Martin is right when he says that right low down we're actually safer. I can't find any way of marking accurately from medium level. Will you let us try this new way on some lightly defended target?"

Cochrane considered for a moment, looked up and said, "All right, we'll give it a trial."

The target he chose was the Gnome-Rhone aero-engine factory at Limoges, 200 miles south-west of Paris. The Germans had taken it over but there was hardly any flak for miles.

There was an immediate complication. War Cabinet vetoed the target because the Germans had 300 French girls working in the factory on night shift and there were French homes near-by. Churchill would not have French people killed if he could possibly avoid it, particularly as this was not a vital target.

Cheshire replied that as far as the homes were concerned he would guarantee they would put all bombs on the target itself. To protect the girls in the factory he offered to make several dummy runs over the factory to give everyone plenty of time to get clear. Cochrane backed him up and, after a silence from Whitehall, permission came through for the raid, on the understanding that if one Frenchman was killed there would be no more.

Twelve aircraft took off into bright moonlight and reached Limoges just before midnight. The town was evidently not expecting bombs because the blackout was bad. Lights showed all over the place and in the factory itself all the workshop lights were on and it was obvious that the Germans had them working hard.

Cheshire dived low and hurtled over the factory at a hundred feet, and as he climbed and turned he saw all the lights vanish. He dived back over it again, and Astbury, his bomb aimer, could see people running below and throwing themselves flat. A third time he dived in warning, and on his fourth run held her down to 50 feet till he was practically scraping the workshop roofs. Astbury called "Bombs gone!" and a cluster of brilliantly glowing incendiaries cascaded into the exact centre of the workshops. In the Lancaster the cameraman filmed it.

Martin dived in the same way and two red spot fires joined the incendiaries. Cheshire called, "Markers dead centre. Bomb as ordered."

At "Zero plus 1" (one minute past midnight) Shannon dropped the first 12,000-pounder from 10,000 feet. It exploded in the middle of the incendiaries and blew them to smithereens but started a big fire that was just as good. In the next eight minutes nine more bombs fell right on the factory, and one fell just outside in the river. The last man, Nicky Ross, had a "hang-up"; his bomb did not release, so he went away and came in on another run. At "Zero plus 18" his 12,000-pounder lobbed in the crater that Shannon's bomb had made.

Cheshire cruised overhead for a while, but there was nothing to see but flames and smoke and soon he turned for home. Apart from two machine guns there was no opposition and none of the Lancasters was holed, not even Cheshire's.

In the morning a recce aircraft brought back pictures which showed that of the factory's forty-eight bays half were scars on the ground and the rest were only shells. A target had never been more completely expunged, and Cheshire knew that, on undefended targets at least, he had proved his point. Cochrane was delighted.

A message reached England from Limoges not long after. The girls of the Gnome-Rhone factory wished to thank the R.A.F. for their considerate warning and would be pleased to welcome the people concerned after the war.

CHAPTER XII

GALLANT FAILURE

IN Italy the Allies were preparing to break out from Anzio and the Germans were preparing to stop them. Trains carrying 15,000 tons of supplies a day were passing over the Antheor Viaduct, and for the third time 617 was ordered to smash it.

Cochrane thought a 12,000-lb. "blockbuster" within 10 yards of the viaduct might knock a span down but this time he warned Cheshire that he must not try "deck-level" marking unless it were absolutely necessary. There were twelve heavy guns and several lighter guns around the viaduct, plus searchlights.

They found the bay at midnight but it was so dark they could not see the viaduct from above 3,000 feet, and as soon as Cheshire and Martin slipped down to that height the flak opened up terrifyingly, nearly twenty guns predicting and concentrating on the two of them. Cheshire made a run to drop his markers, but the searchlights caught him long before he was in position and shells were bursting all round him, so that he had to turn away. Martin tried a run but the same thing happened. Cheshire came in again and jagged lumps of flak ripped holes in his wings and fuselage. He slid out to sea and swung in again, but as he straightened up for the run Martin's voice sounded in his earphones: "Hold off a minute, Leader. I think I'm in position for a low run. I can see everything."

He had dived over the hills inland, was hugging the ridges so that the flak could not see him against the dark mass, and turning down the long ravine that cut down to the viaduct across the bay. When they had looked at the maps at briefing it did not seem possible that an aircraft could get down that way but Martin, who could land a Lancaster out of a steep turn, had his nose dipping into the ravine and could see the viaduct dead ahead, limned against the phosphorescence of the surf on the beach.

Cheshire called back, "O.K. Mick, go ahead."

"Try and draw the flak as long as you can," Martin said. He was deep into the ravine; the viaduct was about a mile in front and some 1,500 feet lower; he throttled his engines back to keep the sound from the guns and at 230 m.p.h. opened his bomb doors and knew he was making the best bombing run he ever had. The guns down by the viaduct were all firing, but their target was Cheshire weaving in towards them from the other side at 4,000 feet.

In the nose of "P Popsie" Bob Hay said over the intercom., "Target markers selected and fused."

"Right," said Martin. "I'm going to level out in the last second."

"O.K." The bomb sight was no use in a dive. Hay relied on Martin for the signal.

The ravine ridges were towering on each side and the viaduct was rushing at them, growing hugely. One gun on the eastern end suddenly swung and out of its muzzle-flashes a chain of shells was swirling at them. Hay called, "Now?" and Martin yelled, "No! No!" He eased the nose up, a second dragged into eternity, he shouted, "Now!" And as he shouted a shell smashed through the nose and exploded in the ammunition trays under the front turret. The aircraft rocked in the crashing din and jagged steel and exploding bullets shot back into the fuselage, hitting flesh and ploughing through hydraulic and pneumatic pipes, control rods and fuse boxes.

Hay must have pressed the button as the bomb release contacts parted, and then they shot a bare couple of feet over the viaduct and dipped towards the water as half a dozen more guns swivelled and spat at them. Foxlee was still alive; for the first time in months he was in the mid-upper turret instead of the nose, and now he was cursing and shooting back, and so was Simpson in the rear. Martin pulled the nose off the water and Whittaker rammed the throttles forward but there was almost no response from the engines.

"P Popsie" was bathed in glare but Simpson and Foxlee put three of the searchlights out with long bursts. They were practically in the water now, and in the glow of the last light Simpson saw the spray hissing up from the prop-wash and thought for a moment it was smoke from a burning engine. Then they were out of range and Martin lifted "P Popsie" a few feet off the water, praying with thankfulness as he found she still had flying speed.

Whittaker leaned over and yelled in his ear, "Port inner and starb'd outer throttles gone and pitch controls for the other two gone." That meant two engines would stay throttled back as they had been for the run down the ravine, and the other two, in fully fine pitch, were straining themselves at maximum revs. on extreme power to keep the aircraft flying.

Martin had felt a sting in his leg as the shell went off and knew he had been hit. He ignored it and began calling the roll round his crew. The tough little Foxlee was all right. Bob Hay did not answer. Whittaker gave him a twisted grin, swearing and hunched, holding his legs. The rest were all right. He called Hay twice more but there was only silence, so he said, "Toby, see if Bob's all right. His intercom. must be busted." Foxlee swung out of his turret and wormed down towards the nose. He lifted his head towards Martin. "He's lying on the floor. Not moving."

Over the viaduct Cheshire was trying to drop his markers but again was coned by searchlights and hit by flak, so he had to stand the Lancaster on a wing-tip and pull her round. He came in again about 3,000 but again he was battered and had to pull away. He climbed to 5,000 but the flak caught him once more.

On his sixth run he dived to upset the predicted flak and

was able to drop flares that lit the viaduct. He turned back for another run and this time the searchlights did not find him. The guns predicted on him but he threaded through them and soon his markers sprang to glowing life as they hit; he saw in the light of the flares that they were on the beach about a hundred yards from the viaduct.

He swung in again with his last two markers, but four seconds short of release point two shells hit "Q Queenie" and she almost stood on her head in the blast. It threw Astbury off his bombing aim, but Cheshire got her back under control and found she would still fly and there was no fire.

The squadron headed in, unable at 10,000 feet to pick up the viaduct from the flares but trying to allow for the error of the markers. One 12,000-pounder went off brilliantly 15 yards from the side of the viaduct, but that was 5 yards too far and the viaduct shook but was not damaged beyond chipping from fragments. Six more exploded a few yards further on and pitted the great stone piers a little more. It was good bombing, but not quite good enough.

Whittaker had taken his tie off and wrapped it round his thigh as a tourniquet. There were a dozen pieces of flak in his legs but the pain was passing into numbness now. He grabbed one of the roof longerons, pulled himself up and found he could stand. Foxlee stuck his head up from the nose and said, "Bob's unconcious. Get a first-aid kit, will you?" Whittaker pulled one of the little canvas bags out of its stowage and eased himself down into the nose. Hay was lying on his side, his head pillowed on the perspex right up in the nose. "Give him some morphia," Foxlee shouted, and Whittaker nodded, unclipped the canvas pack and took out one of the tiny morphia hypodermic tubes. Foxlee unzipped Hay's Irvin jacket sleeve and rolled the battledress sleeve up till Whittaker could see the soft flesh of the forearm, pale in the gloom. He felt the flesh was still warm, jabbed in the needle and squeezed till the tube was empty.

"Let's get him over and see where he's hit," he shouted. Together in the cramped space they edged him over on to his back and Whittaker crawled up and gently turned the head over. He saw the great hole in the side of the head and felt the stickiness in the same moment. He said, "Oh, my God!" and felt he was going to be sick, looked up at Foxlee, but Foxlee was looking down. He had lifted his hand off Hay's chest and the blood showed darkly on his fingers. "He's got it in the chest," he said, and Whittaker said, "Yes, the poor devil's had it."

He crawled back up into the cockpit to his seat beside Martin, leaned over and said, "Bob's dead." Martin looked at him a moment, then looked ahead again and gave a little nod.

Whittaker noticed Kenny Stott, the new navigator, standing by Martin's seat. "Where're we going?" Whittaker said, and Martin gave him a wry little grin. "Somewhere friendly, I hope," he said. "Just been talking it over with Kenny. Got any ideas?"

"Whatever's nearest. How 'bout Gib? Or Sicily? Or North Africa?"

Scott said, "What about Sardinia? Or Corsica? Aren't they closer?"

"Is Corsica ours?" Martin asked, and Whittaker cut in, not sensing then the unconscious humour of it: "Yeah. I saw we got Corsica in the *News of the World* last Sunday."

"O.K. Fair enough. Kenny, give me a course for North Corsica."

Stott went back to his charts and Whittaker said he would try and assess the damage. Martin found "Popsie" had just enough power to claim a little more height, very slowly, so he edged the nose up a little, and soggily, not far from stalling speed, the Lancaster started climbing laboriously. In the darkness she was full of noise, the high-pitched screaming of the two good engines battering at the ears in waves because they would not synchronise properly.

He felt his right foot in the flying boot was wet and remembered he had been hit in the calf. He had enough sense not to strip his leg to investigate because the trouser leg and high flying boot would help staunch the blood. The trouble was, if he lost too much blood, he would pass out and they would all die because no one else could fly "Popsie", particularly the way she was. Against the ragged thrust of the engines the trim would not hold her either straight or level and he was working all the time to keep her flying. With one hand he pulled his tie loose and wrapped it round the calf over the spot where the shrapnel had hit him, knotting it tightly so that it would press the trouser leg against the wound with the effect of half bandage, half tourniquet.

Whittaker came back. "Not too good," he said. "The floor's all smothered in grease. It's from the hydraulics, so you can count them out. Air pressure's gone too."

"I know," Martin said. "I can't get the bomb doors up."

"The CO_2 bottle seems all right," Whittaker said, "so you'll probably be able to get your undercart and flaps down but you won't have any brakes to pull up with."

"Oh!"

"I've kept the best bit to the last," Whittaker said morbidly. "The bomb release fuses have gone for a Burton and we've still got the bombs on board."

"I thought so. That's why she's flying like a brick."

Stott came up with a course for Corsica, and Martin swung on to the new heading. They were about 2,000 feet now.

"We'll have to get rid of the bombs," Stott said. "The fusing circuit's bashed in too, so they must still be fused. We can't unfuse 'em. If you can get high enough I might be able to prod the grips through the floor with a ruler and trip them."

Martin was trying to coax more height out of the stricken plane. He had a 4,000-pounder and several 1,000-pounders in the bomb bays, and the minimum safety height for dropping a 4,000-pounder was 4,000 feet.

Curtis was tapping out a "Mayday" (S.O.S.) and excitedly reported, after a while, he had made contact with Ajaccio in

Above : The extraordinary direct hit on the Saumur tunnel obtained on the first "earthquake bomb" raid, showing how the bomb blew out the mountain over the tunnel. The tiny figures give an idea of the size of the crater.

Below : Shot from inside the Saumur tunnel after the Germans had cleared up the mess in time for the invading armies to take over.

...orking, after the war, on the drawing board where his ideas took shape.

Corsica. An advanced R.A.F. fighter unit had just moved in there and the airfield and flarepath were serviceable.

Foxlee came up from the nose and said in a puzzled voice, "Bob's still warm. His body's quite warm. I think he might be alive." Whittaker went down to investigate and came back up again, a little excited. "He *is* warm," he said. "He *must* be alive still." Martin told Curtis to warn Ajaccio to have a doctor meet them. Curtis made contact again and came back to the cockpit. "They say they haven't got a doctor with any facilities to look after a bad head wound. They say if the kite'll hold together we ought to make for Cagliari. That's in South Sardinia. There's an American bomber base at Elmas Field there, and they've got everything, but it's another hundred and fifty miles."

Martin said feelingly, "What a party! Give me a new course, Kenny." The aircraft was still full of numbing noise; a gale was howling through the shell-hole in the nose and the two good engines still screamed in high pitch. Whittaker was watching his gauges nervously, waiting for the engines to crack under the strain.

They were about 2,700 feet when the stars blotted out and they were in heavy rain, followed soon after by hail. Water was sweeping in through the nose, and then darkness swallowed them as they ran into heavy cloud. It was ice cloud. Martin saw supercooled water droplets filming over the leading edge of the wings, forming the dangerous glazed ice that altered the aerodynamic shape and robbed the wings of lift. He had no spare speed to give him lift, and then the propeller of one of the two good engines slipped right back into coarse pitch and could not be budged out of it. The revs. dropped down to about 1,800; the engine was still giving power but the propeller could not use it all. Martin felt the controls getting soggy; he held on to her, correcting the waffling with great coarse movements, trying to coax her to stay up because Stott was shoving a ruler down through the floor into the bomb bay against the bomb grips. He got a 1,000-pounder away and then the aircraft stalled. Martin couldn't hold her; the nose fell, she squashed down and the starboard wing-tip dropped and they were diving and turning, on the verge of a spin. He had hard left rudder on and the rudder caught her, the spin checked and she was diving, picking up speed. He eased her out but they were down to 1,800 feet. That was clear of the cloud, and soon the thin ice cracked and flicked off the wings. He started climbing again. They still needed 4,000 feet to drop the 4,000-pounder.

It took a long time. At 2,500 feet they were in the ice-cloud again, but Stott prodded two more 1,000-pounders free before the ice started to make "Popsie" soggy again, and this time Martin eased her down out of the cloud before she stalled. He started climbing again and found they were running clear of the worst of the cloud. It was still there, but higher and thinner, and only the barest film of ice seemed to be shining on the wings. "Popsie" slowly gained height, passed the 3,000 mark, but then progress was terribly slow and when at last they reached 3,200 she could not drag herself any higher. She was still at the climbing angle but moving no higher, like an old man trying to climb a fence and not being able to pull himself up.

"She's only squashing along," Martin said. "Can't make the safety height, Kenny. What're our chances if we drop the big one here?"

"Better than trying to land with the thing," Stott said. "Let's give it a go."

He went back to the winch slits in the floor and probed. Martin felt the aircraft jump weakly in the same moment that Stott yelled, "She's gone!" Martin tried to turn away but knew he could not get far enough for safety. The 4,000-pounder took fourteen seconds to fall and it felt like fourteen minutes. The sea below and a little to one side opened up like a crimson rose and almost in the same moment the shock wave hit the aircraft. She jumped like a startled horse and a wing flicked, but Martin caught her smartly with rudder and they were all right.

Curtis came up a couple of minutes later. "Elmas Field

says the best way in is over the mountains in the middle of Sardinia."

"How high are they?" Martin asked. Stott said they were 8,000 feet and Martin showed his teeth sardonically.

They got a landfall on Sardinia about 3.30 a.m. and turned to follow the coast all the way round the south tip, and on e.t.a. Martin let down through light cloud and they came out about 1,000 feet and saw the flarepath.

"Thank God for that," he breathed, and a minute later changed his mind. Elmas was on a narrow spit of land. It had one runway only, a dangerously short one for an emergency landing. Martin steered low over it to see what the overshoot areas were like because they were probably going to need them, and felt a chill as he saw that some genius of an airfield designer had had the fabulous idea of building the runway *across* the spit of land, so that the runway started very abruptly at the beach and stopped just as abruptly and dismayingly quickly at the cliff, where the sea started again. No overshoot.

He still had two 1,000-lb. bombs that Stott could not reach and they were almost certainly fused, so a belly landing was out of the question. With the emergency CO_2 bottle the undercarriage might go down, or it might not; the tyres might be all right or they might have been punctured, and if they were the aircraft stood a good chance of ground-looping so that the undercart would collapse on to the fused bombs. If his first approach was not perfect the aircraft, without brakes, would certainly run over the far cliff. There was not enough power to go round for a second approach.

Whittaker yanked down the handle of the CO_2 bottle, and the undercart swung down and seemed to lock. In the gloom they could not see the tyres. There was just enough pressure left to get some flap down. Martin headed in on a long, low approach, dragging in from miles back, while the crew snugged down at emergency stations. Coming up to the runway he was dangerously low, deliberately, and in the last moment he cut all engines and pulled up the nose to clear the dunes. The speed fell and at about 85 m.p.h. she squashed on the runway about 30 yards from the end, not even bouncing. The undercart held, and as she rumbled on Martin started fish-tailing his rudders. The far cliff was running towards them and he pushed on full port rudder. "Popsie" swung and jolted over the grass verge, slowing more appreciably She started to slew, tyres skidding just short of a ground-loop, and came to a halt 50 yards from the cliff-top.

An ambulance and fire truck had been chasing them along the runway, and a young doctor swung up into the fuselage and they directed him up to the nose. He was out a minute later and said, "I'm sorry, but your buddy's gone. He was dead as soon as it happened."

He went over to Whittaker, lying on the grass, and cut his trouser legs away, exposing the legs messy with blood and torn flesh, and where there was no blood they had a distinct blue tinge. He worked for quarter of an hour on them, dabbing, cleaning and bandaging, while Martin gingerly pulled up his own trouser leg to inspect the damage to himself. The doctor finished bandaging Whittaker and as they loaded him into the ambulance told him, "That's a close call, boy. You nearly lost a leg." He turned to Martin. "Now let's have a look at you," but Martin said as off-handedly as he could, "Don't bother about me, Doc. I'm quite all right."

When he had uncovered his leg he had found one tiny spot of blood on a tiny puncture where a tiny piece of flak, at its last gasp, had just managed to break the skin. It had stung at the time, and imagination had done the rest. The wetness he had felt round his foot was not blood gushing into his flying boot but sweat!

About the same time the rest of the squadron was landing at home (except for Suggitt, who never made it back). Cheshire was lucky. The "erks" found 150 holes in his aircraft.

*   *   *

They buried Bob Hay in Sardinia. Whittaker stayed in hospital while the rest made rough repairs, flew "Popsie" on to Blida, where R.A.F. "erks" did a thorough overhaul, and then flew back to Woodhall Spa, where Cheshire met them with the news that Cochrane had vetoed any more operations for them. "It's no use arguing, Mick," Cheshire said. "He means it. He says you'll only kill yourself if he lets you go on." Martin *did* argue, but Cochrane posted him to 100 Group Headquarters, where he immediately wangled himself on to a Mosquito night-fighter squadron doing "intruder" work over Germany.

I have a letter which Cheshire wrote to a friend some four years after this, talking about the old days. He said: "The backbone of the squadron was Martin, Munro, McCarthy and Shannon, and of these by far the greatest was Martin. He was not a man to worry about administration then (though I think he is now), but as an operational pilot I consider him greater than Gibson, and indeed the greatest that the Air Force ever produced. I have seen him do things that I, for one, would never have looked at."

It is not a bad tribute from a man who has himself often been labelled one of the world's greatest bomber pilots.

CHAPTER XIII

THE MOSQUITO PLAN

COCHRANE was not yet convinced that low level marking was practicable, but he told Cheshire he would lay on more lightly defended targets so the experiment could go on. He wanted the system perfected by the time Wallis's "tallboy" was ready; the first one was nearly ready for testing, and after that they would be some time building up stocks. Meantime the squadron needed some re-forming. With Martin and Suggitt gone there were no flight commanders.

It was Cochrane's idea to split 617 into three flights for easier organisation and training; a happy idea, because it gave Cheshire a chance to promote Shannon, McCarthy and Munro, now the only three of the original squadron left, and all battle-tested, reliable and ideal in temperament and training for 617's unique role.

The squadron had several new pilots now, including another American, Nicky Knilans, a droll youngster from Madison, Wisconsin, with precisely the quality of nervelessness that Cheshire wanted in 617. He had joined the Canadian Air Force before America came into the war and had just recently been transferred. Now a "lootenant" in the U.S. Air Force, he wanted to stay and finish his tour in the R.A.F.

In the next few weeks 617 was busy training new crews and settling down with the new flight commanders. Cheshire and "Talking Bomb" kept flying around at 5,000 feet trying medium-level marking, but could find no way of lining-up an indistinct target. Cochrane told them to keep trying.

The first couple of prototype "tallboys" were finished, and

at Ashley Walk range, in the New Forest, the complicated process of testing them started. They were sinister objects, 21 feet long, shining blue-black steel, slim and perfectly stream-lined, weighing 12,030 lb. A Lancaster dropped one on test from 20,000 feet, and it sliced through the air like a bullet till it was falling faster than a bomb had ever fallen before. Long before it hit it passed the speed of sound, and as the com-pressed waves of the sonic barrier piled up round it the bomb vibrated in flight so that it almost toppled and was deflected slightly from its even course, just enough to interfere with the fanatical accuracy that Wallis wanted.

He overcame it with a brilliant idea, offsetting the tail fins so that, as the next bomb dropped and gathered speed, the offset fins began to revolve it. Faster and faster it whirled till by the time it reached the speed of sound it was spinning like a high-speed top, and the gyroscopic action held it perfectly steady as it plunged through the sonic barrier.

At Ashley Walk they dropped one with dummy filling from 20,000 feet and it sank 90 feet into the earth, almost enough for the maximum camouflet that Wallis had planned from 40,000 feet, and certainly enough to make a respectable earthquake.

Came the day of dropping the first "live" one, and they buried a movie camera in the earth to film it. There was some discussion as to where the camera should go, and perhaps it was logical (if a little cynical) that they decided to bury it right in the centre of the white circle that was the target, on the assumption that it was the safest spot.

The result was a lesson for anyone who doubted Wallis's genius. Peering over the edge of the sandbagged dug-out half a mile away, they saw the slim shape streak down and hit the centre of the target, right on the camera! The dug-out trembled, and where the camera had been was a smoking, stinking crater eighty feet deep and a hundred feet across.

Cochrane called Cheshire to Group H.Q. and told him the earthquake bomb had passed its tests with honours and they were now building up stocks for "a big operation" in the spring and summer.

Cheshire had been pondering some new marking ideas. It seemed to him that Lancasters were too big and clumsy for marking; too big a target for the flak and too clumsy for manœuvring low over rough ground on pin-point targets. He went to Cochrane and suggested that he try marking in a Mosquito, and Cochrane liked the idea. The twin-engined Mosquito was much faster as well as smaller and "nippier". Provided Mosquitoes could be used, Cochrane for the first time began to feel more comfortable about the idea of sending crews out to mark at low level.

A new idea was already growing in Cochrane's mind: to have 617 mark for the whole of his Group, about twelve squadrons, instead of the Pathfinders. He had already sounded out Harris on his new idea and Harris had reacted favourably. Cochrane reasoned that if they could show that low marking in Mosquitoes was reasonably safe, Harris would probably give 5 Group its chance. He said to Cheshire:

"Well, I'll see if I can get you a couple of Mosquitoes, and then I'd like you to try them first on easy targets. If it seems all right, you could have a go at a tough one."

It was not easy for Cochrane to get hold of Mosquitoes for 617. They were in short supply and great demand. While he was working on this, 617 visited the explosives factory at Bergerac, on the banks of the Dordogne.

For once, in the light of flares, Cheshire's bomb aimer, Astbury, got a good sight at 5,000 feet and put his markers on the factory. Munro did the same. Shannon and McCarthy branded the explosives dump near-by, and Bunny Clayton put a 12,000-pounder in the middle of the dump. For fifteen seconds it looked as though the sun was coming up underneath; five minutes later the factory as well as the dump was a sea of flame. No bomb fell outside the works.

A pleased Cochrane rang Cheshire next day. "Pack your over-night bag," he said. "You're coming down with me to see Air Chief Marshal Harris about a couple of Mosquitoes."

That night they dined with Harris in his house near High Wycombe. Over the port Harris suddenly said, "Cheshire, what makes you think you can mark from nought feet in a Mosquito and get away with it?"

"There's no question that we can mark accurately, sir. The only thing is having a reasonable chance in the face of heavy opposition. Air Vice-Marshal Cochrane thinks a Lancaster is too big and slow. Against heavy opposition I'm inclined to think now he is right, but I believe he agrees with me that the chances in a Mosquito are good. I believe in a Mosquito we can have a go at any target under the sun and mark with under twenty yards accuracy."

"I've always wanted to bomb Munich properly, and I've never succeeded," Harris said. "It's got four hundred guns. D'you think you could mark that on the deck and get away with it?"

"Yes, sir. I do."

Cochrane cut in, saying that they should practise first with the Mosquito on less lethal targets so they would know precisely what was possible.

"All right," Harris said, "I'll see if I can get you two Mosquitoes . . . just on loan for a month. If by that time you can mark Munich accurately for me, you can keep them."

Just behind Calais the Germans had started work again on the bomb-proof rocket and long-range gun bases. Thousands of slaves were crawling over the massive blockhouses and it was obvious that the secret-weapon project was nearing completion again. Whitehall knew now that the weapon was to fall on London and the invasion ports, but kept it very secret. If the secret weapons started up before the invasion and the R.A.F. could not destroy the blockhouses, London would be destroyed and it was likely that the invasion would also be wrecked.

Churchill was insisting on twice-daily Intelligence reports. Some reports put the weight of the secret-weapon warhead as high as 10 tons of explosive and suggested they might fall at a rate of thousands a week. Churchill ordered the preparation of plans for the evacuation of London and told Sir Arthur Harris that the blockhouses were to be destroyed without fail before they were ready for action.

Wallis's "tallboy" was the only weapon Harris knew of that might smash them, but the "tallboys" would not be ready for some time. They would have to be dropped from at least 18,000 feet to get enough speed for penetration, and only one squadron could drop them accurately enough. But the sites would be so well camouflaged in the bomb-pocked earth that a bomb aimer would have trouble getting them in his bomb sight from 18,000 feet even by day. Though the sites were fairly plastered with flak they would have to be marked clearly and with unprecedented accuracy because there would be no "tallboys" to waste. It was a pretty problem, and Harris called the Pathfinder chief, Bennett, and Cochrane and Cheshire to a conference at his headquarters.

Bennett said frankly that the Pathfinders were not equipped to mark with such accuracy, and Cochrane suggested that 617 might be able to do the marking as well as the bombing.

Cheshire said: "I doubt if it could be marked accurately at medium level. You'd have to run-up straight and level, and at that height the searchlights would blind you so you couldn't see the target, and the flak would pretty surely get you anyway. I should think, sir, we could mark it at very low level in a diving attack."

Cochrane said warningly, "Not in a Lancaster."

"No, sir. In a Mosquito, as we discussed before. She's so fast we could be in and out before the defences could nail us."

A day later Cochrane phoned Cheshire: "I've got two Mosquitoes for you. They're over at Colby Grange. Go and learn to fly them and be quick about it. Let me know as soon as you're ready to use them."

Cheshire was delighted with the Mosquitoes, and within two days felt at home in them. The only possible fault he could find was that, carrying a load of heavy markers, their range might be a little short for some of the more distant targets. Munich, for instance, would be barely within range, so he asked Group to get him some long-range drop tanks as soon as possible.

Signs of the squadron's growing prestige were not lacking. March brought them nine more decorations; popular ones. Among them were a Bar for Martin's D.S.O., a second Bar for Cheshire's D.S.O., a Bar for Whittaker's D.F.C., and the D.F.C. to add to Foxlee's D.F.M.

Cheshire flew down to Weybridge to see Wallis about tactics for dropping the "tallboys".

"I haven't really designed this thing for concrete," Wallis said, "so I think, my dear boy, it might not be a good thing to drop them right on the roofs of those wretched concrete affairs; they might bounce out again like corks. However, you needn't worry; just drop them down at the side in the earth and they'll bore down and blow them up from underneath." He stuck pins in a diagram to show the vulnerable points and added disapprovingly, "The Germans are very silly not to put twenty feet of concrete *under* these things, not on top."

Cheshire suggested as tactfully as he could that, though he had enormous faith in his squadron, it was one thing to stick pins in a diagram and another to drop a bomb in that spot from 20,000 feet.

"Oh well," Wallis said huffily, "if I'd known you propose to scatter the bombs around the countryside like grass seed I'd never have bothered to design them."

CHAPTER XIV

THE UNAPPEASING OF MUNICH

ON April 4 Cheshire reported to Cochrane that he was ready with the Mosquito. Cochrane rang Harris and asked permission for his whole group to operate by themselves, led by 617 to mark the target, which was to be a large aircraft factory just outside Toulouse. Harris agreed, and next night they took off.

Cheshire found his Mosquito handled delightfully. A flare force lit up the factory and Cheshire dived fast and low over it, but, not satisfied with his positioning, pulled up sharply without dropping his markers. Heavy flak opened up on him as he corkscrewed away. He would almost certainly have been hit in a Lancaster, but the shells did not even scratch the Mosquito's paint. He dived again, once more was not satisfied and pulled up in a hail of shells. The third time his markers fell in the centre of the buildings, and again he climbed steeply away, unscathed. At 10,000 feet the squadrons moved in. Munro put an 8,000-pounder right on the markers and the rest of the bombs slathered the spot.

In the morning a recce aircraft found the factory flattened and only an occasional crater in the fields beyond.

Four days later 617 continued the experiment, going alone, led by Cheshire in the Mosquito, to attack the biggest German air park and signals depot in France, at St. Cyr, some two miles west of Versailles. Cheshire put his nose nearly straight down from 5,000 feet, let his markers go from 700, and they lobbed on the western corner of the target. He ordered the bombers in and soon rolling coils of smoke hid the target.

Cheshire landed as dawn was breaking and found Cochrane

in the de-briefing room; he had been waiting up all night to see how the raid went and took Cheshire aside.

"That's the end of the experiment, Cheshire. I'm satisfied you can do it low in Mosquitoes now, and we're going to start thinking of the big targets. I'm getting you four new Mosquitoes. Train three or four picked pilots to use them and be quick about it."

The four Mosquitoes arrived that afternoon, and in the next six days McCarthy, Shannon, Kearns and Fawke spent their waking hours flying them. They were to fly Mosquitoes exclusively from now on and their crews were split up. Shannon kept the tough Sumpter as his navigator. Danny Walker stayed as squadron navigation officer, Goodale went off for a well-deserved rest, and Buckley joined another crew. The lanky and good-natured Concave had won a D.F.C. and Bar as a wireless operator, which is not far short of a miracle, because decorations for good work by a crew usually went first to the pilot, then to the navigator and bomb aimer. Or to a gunner who shot enemy aircraft down, or an engineer who had a chance to keep battered engines going in the air. A wireless operator had little chance.

Decorations were a vexed question because there was no way of equitable distribution. Cheshire had strong views on the subject; as usual, unorthodox views but extraordinarily perceptive. Generally he divided courageous aircrews into two categories: (a) men with acute imagination who realised they would probably die and who forced themselves to go on, and (b) men who, though intelligent, could shut their minds off from imagination and carry on without acute forebodings of the future. Cheshire puts himself in the second group and, typically, regards the first group as the braver men.

"That's the highest form of courage," he said once. "They have a hell of a time but keep going. Usually they're not the spectacular types and they don't win the flash awards, but they're the bravest."

He told me once: "Decorations are not particularly a test of courage but a test of success. There aren't many awards for failure; a few, but not many, no matter what bravery was shown."

On April 18 Cheshire reported to Cochrane that the Mosquito crews were all ready, and that night 617 marked for 5 Group againt Juvisy marshalling yards, eleven miles south of Paris.

Munro's flares lit the area beautifully: Cheshire, Fawke, Shannon and Kearns dived to 400 feet and lobbed their spot fires into the middle of the web of rails, though one bounced outside. It all went like clockwork. 617 bombed the spot fires accurately, as usual, and then the rest of 5 Group, 200 Lancasters, surged in and excelled themselves. They were used only to area bombing and not precision bombing, but this time, with the bright aiming points of the markers, they put nearly all their bombs in the target area. Some fell outside on the marker that bounced but morning reconnaissance showed the ragged end of rails in acres of erupted earth where a thousand craters overlapped each other. (It was eighteen months after the war before the yard was again in action.)

From the spot fire that bounced, Cheshire learned the importance of releasing the markers before the Mosquitoes started to flatten out of the dive, and that was another step towards perfection of the technique.

Once again 617 lost no aircraft and the Mosquitoes did not have a single hole among them. To Cheshire and Cochrane—and to Harris too—it was further confirmation of their ideas.

Cochrane flew to Woodhall, saw Cheshire privately in Cheshire's office and, as usual, wasted no words:

"Now you can have a crack at Germany. Tomorrow you're going to Brunswick . . . One Group as well as Five Group, so you'll be leading about four hundred aircraft. Pathfinders will drop flares and you'll mark with red spots."

There was one alternative, he said. If cloud hid the target, special radar Pathfinders would mark "blind" with green spots instead.

*   *   *

The first P.F.F. flares went down over Brunswick, but Cheshire could see no target (rail yards) by their light. More flares went down seven miles north, and over that spot Kearns and Fawke saw the target and dropped their red spots "on the button". Cheshire gave the order to bomb, and the first bombs were just exploding when the reserve radar Pathfinders ran into cloud near-by and dropped their green spots on fields three miles away. Most of the main force, according to orders, turned for them.

Cheshire called till he was blue in the face, but the radio was jammed and only a few aircraft picked up his message. Nearly all the bombs fell on the wrong markers out in the fields.

After they landed back at Woodhall, Cochrane flew over in his Proctor and Cheshire started apologising for the mix-up. Cochrane cut in:

"All right, Cheshire. Don't you worry about that. You did your part perfectly. We've learned a bit more from it and we'll see the trouble doesn't happen again. How do you feel about Munich?"

"As soon as you like, sir. We're ready."

"I've been on to Air Chief Marshal Harris. If the weather is all right you're going tomorrow night, leading the whole group again. You'll go for the rail yards."

Together they planned it, and this time it looked as though it could not miss. Bomber Command was to raid Karlsruhe half an hour before to draw the fighters. 617 was to lead 5 Group towards Switzerland as a feint; six Lancasters were to swerve south towards Milan dropping bundles of "window" (thin strips of metal foil) to delude German radar into thinking 5 Group was heading for Italy. Just before the Group reached Munich, radar Pathfinders were to drop flares, and Cheshire and the Mosquitoes were to mark, the rest of 617 were to drop more markers from medium level with the S.A.B.S. in case the early markers were blown out, and then the 200 Lancasters were to bomb.

One point worried Cheshire. "Munich is about as far as a

Mosquito can get without overload tanks," he said. "I've asked for them but they haven't come yet. We're not going to have enough margin for bad winds or upset timing without them."

"Give Group a sharp nudge about them," Cochrane said. "I'm going down to the C.-in-C. with the plan."

Cheshire phoned Group, and they said they would do all they could. He phoned them again next morning and was dismayed when they told him the tanks were in acutely short supply and other Mosquito units had priorities.

Cheshire got hold of Pat Kelly, his navigator, and they worked out a new plan for the Mosquitoes: to fly first to Manston, in Kent, a hundred miles nearer the target, pour in all the petrol they could and fly straight to Munich across all the defences. Kelly plotted the distance, worked out their range from Manston and looked up grimly.

"If everything goes dead to time—which I've seldom seen —and if the winds are all in our favour—which I've never seen—we might just get back, but probably won't."

Cheshire went to a high officer at base and explained respectfully that, even taking off from Manston, he doubted if the four marking Mosquitoes would get back. It was usual to have a couple of hours' petrol in reserve—at least—to allow for contingencies. With the very best conditions they might arrive back with a few minutes' petrol. Personally he had never had to fly on a raid in such conditions. Nor did he know anyone who did. What should he do?

The answer was not inspiring.

"If you can't do this marking in Mosquitoes," the high officer said, "you'll have to do it in a Lancaster. Whatever you do the raid has to go on."

Cheshire said, "Yes, sir."

He went back and collected the four Mosquito crews. They got a preliminary Met. report: heavy cloud—possible ice cloud—over the western half of Germany; perhaps clear over Munich. At 14,000 feet the winds might be reasonably

The *Tirpitz* lying capsized in Tromso Fiord. Alongside her are salvage vessels.

Above: A ten-ton "Grand Slam" being taken from the bomb dump.

Below: The Bielefeld Viaduct, showing the flooded craters made by months of futile bombing and, in the shadow of the viaduct, the huge crater made by the first "Grand Slam", which brought it down.

favourable. The four navigators bent over their calculations and looked up grimly.

Kelly said, "If everything goes perfectly we might get back to Manston." They all knew that a raid rarely went perfectly.

One of them exploded: "Hell sir, we don't mind sticking our necks out over the defences. That's just part of the job, but we can't see any point in such an unnecessary risk. What sort of fools are we supposed to be?"

Cheshire said, "I'm sorry, but we've got to go." There was a brief silence and one of them said, "All right."

The four Mosquitoes flew down to Manston and were re-fuelled and parked at take-off point so they would waste no fuel taxi-ing. Sitting silently over dinner with the others, Cheshire got a phone call from Cochrane.

"I'm deeply sorry about the overload tanks," Cochrane said. "Can you make it?"

"We'll have a go, sir. I think it will be all right."

"I just want to let you know," Cochrane said, "I've had a word with the C.-in-C. When you get back he's giving the whole squadron a week's leave."

Cheshire went and told the others, and Kelly said acidly, "Fat lot of good that's going to do *us*." Cheshire had never seen them like that. They seemed almost on the verge of mutiny, not because they were too scared (they were scared all right, but so is nearly every airman before a raid), but this time it *was* unnecessary.

Around dusk Cheshire said, "Well, let's get it over." They walked out silently; it was clear over England, the sun dipping under the horizon and the sky above flaming orange. Cheshire said, "What a glorious sunset!" From the others a sullen silence, and then Shannon, without even lifting his eyes towards the west, said, "Damn the sunset. I'm only interested in the sun*rise*."

They took off without warming up, climbed straight on course to 14,000 feet and over the North Sea ran into heavy cloud.

* * *

They were coming up to the Rhine. Or hoped they were. Cloud lay on the earth like a deep, drifting ocean, rolling up unbroken to 17,000 feet, and in the hooded glow of the cockpits each pilot found comfort in the dim shape of his navigator beside him, feeling they were outcasts sealed in a small world. Beyond the numbing thunder of engines lay nothing but blackness and they only sensed that somewhere in a few square miles of sky they were together, unseen. Cheshire broke radio silence to ask Shannon how he was finding the weather and felt his scalp prickle as a voice out of the past spoke in his earphones, "Is that you, sir?" He recognised it instantly, through the static and the careful anonymity . . . Micky Martin.

He called back, "Is that you, Mick?"

"Yessir."

"Where on earth *are* you?"

"Oh, I'm around."

"What the hell are you doing?"

"Sticking my neck out for you types."

(Martin was a hundred miles away in another Mosquito, a night fighter, his job being to "beat up" German night fighter fields, encouraging the fighters to stay on the ground while the bombers plastered Karlsruhe and Munich; another part of Cochrane's planning.)

One wastes no time in radio chatter over enemy soil. Plotting stations need few seconds for a "fix". Cheshire said, "Good luck to you, Mick," and Martin answered laconically, "Good luck to you too. Be seeing you."

The other Mosquitoes heard it and flew on a little more cheerfully. It seemed an omen somehow, but whether for good or bad they were not quite sure.

Apparently it was for good! The clouds thinned, winds stayed kind and exactly on zero hour they came out over Munich. No mistaking it; the flare force had arrived and massed guns were vomiting upwards. At 14,000 feet the flashes of bursts split the night and lines of red balls were marching up from the lighter guns. There must have been a hundred searchlights; pale fingers probing the dark, lighting now and then on aircraft which glinted like ants and turned to burrow into the crevices of the night. Mostly they vanished, but one was caught in a second beam, and a third. They saw it coned and held as it dived and turned and climbed, a trapped little ant. The flak hunted it; in the glare they saw the brighter flashes all round and then the ribbon of flame as the Lancaster dived again; this time the nose never lifted.

A flare abruptly glowed in the darkness, then another, a third—five . . . one by one they lit till thirty hung flaming in the sky over the naked city, so that Cheshire recognised from the photographs the kidney-shaped park, the long lake, drilled streets of pygmy houses and the lined acres of the rail yards. He shouted over the R/T, "Marker Leader going in" and peeled off from 10,000 feet, holding the nose down till the little Mosquito was moving into the flak faster than she had ever travelled. Sliding past 5,000 feet he lined her up on the rail yards, focused his mind on them, still aware in a curiously detached way of shells, balloon cables and searchlight dazzle, hoped he would miss them and coldly shut his mind to them. The little plane was shivering with the headlong surge and the busy fury of the engines; Cheshire barely heard the screaming noise: she was twisting in the rising speed against the trim and he was coaxing her to arrow dead straight in the dive, forcing himself to wait for the dragging seconds till he suddenly jabbed the bomb button and eased back on the stick. He felt her lifting out instantly, the mounting "g" ramming him hard down into his seat, a phantom load dragging at his lips, his cheeks, his eyeballs and his blood, heavier and heavier, till his vision was greying out as the Mosquito flattened low over the roof-tops, curved up and climbed nimbly away. He let her lift into the darkness over the flares before he rolled her out on one wing, looked over the side and saw his markers, two red eyes glowing in the rail yards.

Shannon dived in the same way and put his markers within a hundred yards of Cheshire's. Kearns did likewise. Cheshire called the 617 Lancasters, told them to back up, and minutes later their clusters of incendiaries splashed into brightness on the rail yards.

It was the spearhead that Bomber Command had never had over Munich; even the giant flashes from the 8,000-pounders and the coils of smoke soon rolling over the rail yards did not hide the pin-points of the markers, and the bomb aimers made the most of it.

The destruction was not all on one side. Cheshire several times saw the trails of flame, like shooting stars, streaking for the ground and the explosions when they hit. It was the flak that caused most of them. Nearly all the fighters had been sent to Karlsruhe or down to Milan, and few had enough petrol to fly back to Munich.

Petrol shortage or not, Cheshire flew full throttle round and round the inner city at 1,000 feet, checking the accuracy and ready to call up with new instructions if the bombing looked like moving off the target area. The gunners below could hear him and the searchlights and flak chased him, but the Mosquito was too fleet. Once a beam held him for a second and destroyed his night vision, but he was too fast to hold low down and passed into darkness again. Light flak exploded around him; he heard the crack of the shells and the aircraft shook from near misses. A dozen lumps of shrapnel gashed it and hit the engines but hurt no vital spot.

Satisfied he could do no more he turned for home; the other Mosquitoes were already on their way. It was not a happy trip back; no flak or fighters to speak of, but Kelly doing intricate petrol calculations, thumbing the fuel gauge, plotting his track and e.t.a., and trying to look philosophical. It seemed the longest trip they had ever made, and then they came in over Manston with ten minutes' petrol on the gauges. Some gauges on low tanks are as reliable as a woman's intuition. They might have petrol for ten minutes, or fifteen minutes, or ten seconds, and were going to need at least five minutes for approach, circuit and landing.

Throttled right back in coarse pitch, Cheshire flicked his navigation lights on and dipped his nose towards the long runway, where the flarepath shone like a stolid but comforting guard of honour. Kelly said: "What's wrong with their runway? Look at those funny lights down there." Cheshire looked . . . puzzled. There *were* lights blinking in and out of the flarepath. "Funny," he said. It hit him suddenly and shouted to Kelly, "Turn those navigation lights off. It's a Jerry fighter."

The target, they found out later, was Gerry Fawke, just settling down on the runway. The fighter had stalked him round the circuit and gone for the kill when Fawke had his flaps, undercart and speed right down and was helpless, unable to turn sharply—unless he wanted to stall and spin in. Luck, it seemed, stayed with 617 that night. The German fighter, with a "sitter" in front of his guns, missed completely. Fawke rolled to a stop and the flarepath flicked off. Cheshire made a careful approach, took a quick sight at the last moment with his landing lights and set his aircraft down safely. In the briefing room he found the other Mosquito crews. None had got down with more than fifteen minutes' petrol to spare (a terrifyingly small margin).

Shannon said, "Wake me at sunrise. I want to see it."

Back at Woodhall later in the morning, they found the 617 Lancasters all back except Cooper. No one ever found out where Cooper went down. Cochrane flew over, showing what was, for him, extravagant delight, a wide but faintly embarrassed smile, as he congratulated and thanked them. He said to Cheshire, "You might like to look at this." It was an aerial photograph of Munich, brought back by recce Mosquito an hour earlier. Round a couple of scars on the outskirts were circles of ink, and Cochrane tapped the spots with his finger. "That's how it was up to yesterday afternoon after all the other raids." He put his finger on the cratered rail yards. "Last night," Cochrane said. "It seems to justify us."

The photograph staggered even Cheshire, who knew what

the bombing had been like. There must have been a hundred times more damage in that one raid than the dozen previous ones, especially as the previous damage had been on no significant target. This time they had struck an effective blow.

It proved Cheshire's contention that he could mark a heavily defended target at low level without undue risk, but the photograph also showed that one solitary marker from the high force had fallen outside the target area and drawn some of the bombs, so that a lot of houses were either gutted shells or mounds of rubble. Unfortunate though that was, it led to further improvement in the marking technique. Cochrane and Cheshire had both thought it too dangerous to rely on one marker only, since it might be obscured by smoke or hit by a bomb. Now they realised that dropping too many markers could also be risky, and thereafter they tended to cut the number of markers down to try and eliminate such accidents as the one stray marker at Munich.

On the strength of Munich, Cochrane drove down to see Harris and asked for four extra Mosquitoes so that another of his squadrons could learn the 617 way of target marking.

Harris, who never did things by halves, said, "Not four Mosquitoes, Cocky"; and almost before Cochrane could feel his disappointment Harris went on, "I'm sending you a squadron of Mosquitoes from Pathfinders and two Pathfinder Lancaster squadrons. You can operate as a group by yourselves now. Get 617 to teach the new Mosquitoes low marking, and then they can mark for your group, with the two Lanc. squadrons as flare force. That'll release 617 for some special jobs."

CHAPTER XV

EARTHQUAKE BOMB

COCHRANE sent for Cheshire and took him walking in the grounds of headquarters away from listening ears.

"You'll be doing no more operations for a month," he said, "and then you'll be doing a very special one. You'll spend the next month training for it."

He would say no more, but next day a scientist, Dr. Cockburn, arrived at Woodhall from London and also took Cheshire walking. They lay alone on the grass by the air field, obviously for privacy. Cockburn said: "I understand you can be trusted to keep your mouth shut, so I'm going to tell you something a lot of Cabinet Ministers and generals don't know yet. You know by now an invasion is coming off very soon. If the weather is right it will be in about a month, and landings will be made west of Le Havre. We want to fool the Germans we're going in somewhere else."

Cheshire waited.

"On that night," Cockburn went on, "there's going to be a big convoy fourteen miles wide passing across the Channel at seven knots."

"Sounds a pretty big invasion," Cheshire said.

"That isn't the invasion. They'll be heading towards Cap d'Antifer, on the other side of Le Havre."

"A diversion!"

"Yes."

"I must say," Cheshire said, "it sounds a pretty big diversion. Have they got all those ships to spare?"

"No. They won't be ships. They'll be you and your boys."

Cheshire rolled over and looked at him. "Us!" he said blankly and then got the glimmerings of an idea. "Dropping window?"

"That's it," said Cockburn. "It's going to need the most precise flying you've ever done. Can you do this . . . can you all fly in a very wide formation, invisible to each other, and do a lot of intricate manœuvring, keeping within three seconds of all your e.t.a.'s and within twenty feet of your height."

"I don't know. Doesn't sound very possible."

"It'll have to go on for hours and hours," Cockburn said, "so you'll do it in two waves. Eight aircraft for a few hours and then the second eight taking over from them." He went on to explain the technique: lines of aircraft a set distance apart, flying precise courses at precise speeds and height, throwing out window at intervals of a precise number of seconds. The planes would fly thirty-five seconds on course, turn evenly, fly a reverse course for thirty-two seconds, a slow turn again back to the first course and start throwing out more window. They would thus start the original course again at a point slightly ahead of where the previous one started and the first of the new lot of window would drop from the aircraft at the moment that the first bundle dropped on the previous leg hit the water, so there would be no interruption of the steady blips on German radar. It would go on like that for eight hours, timed to give an effect of a large convoy several rows of ships deep moving at seven knots towards the French coast.

The training never let up except for one day when the weather closed in. Otherwise there was no moment, night or day, in the next month when some 617 aircraft were not flying, particularly by night, cruising at a steady 200 m.p.h. on a steady course and height, curving in even turns to reverse courses, turning back on the stop watch, unspectacular, tedious and demanding meticulous care and skill.

They all sensed the invasion was drawing near; Cheshire had the idea that the Germans might drop paratroops on British airfields on D-day, so he persuaded Doc Watson's armament section to issue as many aircrew as they could with either a revolver, Sten gun, rifle or hand grenade. It was one of his few sad mistakes. For three days life was a precarious possession at Woodhall. First they set dinner plates up on the lawn near the mess and loosed off at them with Sten guns from the second-floor windows. That palled after a while, so they started lobbing hand grenades in the general direction of the sergeants' mess. At night time Buckley became a terrible menace, keeping a vigil by his bedroom window and loosing off clips from his Sten gun over the heads of late home-comers so that they had to crawl to bed over the back lawn on their bellies.

Even Witherick, who was known to be too durable for death by any of the known methods of war, commented uncomfortably, "The only time you're safe on this squadron is when you're in the air!" It became obvious that German paratroops were less of a menace than the local aircrew army, so Cheshire collected all the weapons and returned them to the armoury. Peace descended once more on the mess, to the regret of Shannon and McCarthy. Shannon and McCarthy were rarely seen apart; they drank together and dined together and it was logical, therefore, that they should act together to revive the reign of terror, climbing to the roof of squadron headquarters to drop a Véry cartridge down the adjutant's chimney. They knew the innocent Humphries had a fire in the grate.

A Véry cartridge in artful hands is like a semi-lethal firework; exploding in a confined space it resembles a small but concentrated bombing raid, providing a monstrous crash, sheets of coloured flame and clouds of choking smoke. Half the beauty of the thing is that it goes on for about fifteen seconds. They dropped it down the chimney and started laughing as the waves of sound came rocking up from below.

Unfortunately it was not Humphries' chimney, but the commanding officer's. Cheshire scuttled out, pursued by flashes and rolling fumes, ran on to the tarmac and spotted his two flight commanders hiding behind a chimney. With aristocratic dignity he said nothing but for several nights Shannon and McCarthy found themselves doing duty officer together, an irksome task which kept them out of their beds and abstemiously patrolling the station buildings.

Throwing Véry cartridges into the mess fire had long been a favourite sport, so Cheshire thought it time to issue a stern order that no firearms, cartridges or pyrotechnics of any kind be brought into the mess building.

He was woken that night by a scuttling outside his window, threw it wide open and saw a rat running across the roof. Quick as lightning he grabbed his own .38 revolver from his dressing-table and took a pot-shot that bowled the rat over and echoed through the quiet night like a small cannon. Cheshire was still leaning out of his window, revolver in hand, when the next window shot open and the head of Danny Walker poked out. "Got the dirty rat that time," Cheshire said triumphantly and became conscious of Walker's eyes staring coldly, focusing on the hand that held the gun. He felt his face going red and ducked inside, laying the pistol down, and heard Walker's voice next door, talking loudly to a mythical room-mate, "But I tell you, old boy, I distinctly heard the man say that *no* one under *any* circumstances was to have a firearm inside the mess."

On June 5 everyone was confined to camp, and at dusk, with guards on the doors of the briefing room, Cheshire told the crews that the invasion was about to start. The first wave of eight planes took off about 11 p.m. with twelve men in each aircraft, an extra pilot, extra navigator and three men to drop the bundles of window out.

They made absolutely no mistakes that night, though it would have taken an error of only four seconds in timing to make the convoy suspiciously change position on the German radar. Hour after hour they flew in the blackness over the Channel, turning on stop-watches up and down on reversed courses while the window was tossed out at four-second intervals. Round 3 a.m. the second wave of eight aircraft took over, the trickiest part of all because they had to come in directly behind with split-second timing to carry on. They saw nothing of the invasion.

They were to break away just before dawn, before the light was good enough for the Germans to see from the shore that they had been tricked. By that time they should be within seven miles of the French coast, and that is exactly where they were. Farther north another squadron was doing a similar task with at least as much success.

They had their reward as they turned for home; the German coastal batteries opened up . . . not the flak but the big guns, aiming 12-inch shells by radar prediction at the ghost armada. German E-boats came out from Calais and Boulogne but they would have needed aerial torpedoes to do any damage.

It is history now that the Germans really thought the main invasion was aiming at that area. (In prison camp in the heart of Germany that day, I heard the German radio announcing two huge armadas heading in towards Cap d'Antifer and Calais. It gave us great joy, but we wondered for months what had happened to those convoys.)

Inland from Boulogne and Dieppe the bulk of the German Army, which should have been hurrying to the real invasion area on the other side of Le Havre, waited . . . and waited, poised to swoop on the armadas that were not there. By the time the Germans woke up to it other squadrons had blasted bridges over the Seine between them and the invasion and the Allied troops were consolidating their landings with greater freedom from counter-attack than they had dreamed possible.

Cheshire was driving round the perimeter track with Munro that evening for no particular reason that he can remember, and just past the A Flight hardstandings they passed a huge tarpaulin-covered lorry cruising slowly along.

"What's that doing here?" Munro murmured, not very curiously, and Cheshire, his head still full of D-Day precautions, said, "Lord knows. Let's find out."

They drove across the lorry's bows; it stopped and they

climbed out of their jeep and went back to the lorry driver. "What have you got in there?" Cheshire asked.

"Boilers for the cookhouse, sir," the driver said.

"Aren't you going the wrong way? The cookhouse is over there," Cheshire waved a hand to the rear.

"Well I dunno, sir. They told me to deliver them over there." The driver pointed to the far side of the field.

"The bomb dump! That's the bomb dump. Who told you that?" A suspicious edge had crept into Cheshire's voice.

"That's what they told me, sir."

Cheshire said, "Let's have a look at this, Les. Something funny here." He heaved himself over the tailboard of the lorry. Another tarpaulin covered a shapeless bulk in the back; he tugged a corner clear and, unbidden, a grunt of surprise came out of him. "Look at these!"

Lashed to the floor were two shining steel monsters. They were like sharks, slim, streamlined and with sharp noses. "Bombs," Cheshire said, almost in awe. "Wallis's 'tallboys'."

They followed the lorry to the bomb dump and were staggered to find the dump nearly full of "tallboys", snugged down under tarpaulins. An armament officer said apologetically, "They've been coming in at night time for the past week, sir. I was told to keep quiet about them."

Cheshire tore back to his office, got Cochrane at Group on the secret scrambled phone and told him he had just been inspecting "the new boilers for the cookhouse in the bomb dump." He heard what sounded like the ghost of muted amusement in Cochrane's voice:

"Just see they're safely in storage, Cheshire. You'll be using them soon."

The call came without warning forty-eight hours later. Intelligence had reported a German panzer division moving up from Bordeaux by rail to attack the invasion. The trains would have to pass through the Saumur Tunnel, near the Loire, over a hundred miles inland, and in the late afternoon

Harris suggested to Cochrane that they might have a chance of blocking the tunnel before the trains reached it. They would have to move fast; it would be nightfall before bombers could reach the spot, and a tunnel on a dark night would be an elusive pin-point of a target. Only one squadron could do it; that was obvious. And probably only one type of bomb!

Cheshire got the order about 5 p.m. to take off as soon as they could, and there was a mad rush to collect everyone, trolley the "tallboys" out of the dump and winch them up into the bomb bays. They were airborne soon after dusk, and it was shortly after midnight that Cheshire, in his Mosquito, dropped flares by a bend of the river and saw where the rails vanished into the tunnel that led under the Saumur hill.

He dive-bombed from 3,000 feet, aimed his red spots point blank, and as he pulled up from about a hundred feet saw them lying beautifully in the tunnel mouth. Ninety seconds later the Lancasters were steady on their bombing runs, and a couple of minutes later the first earthquake bombs ever dropped on business were streaking down.

Ten thousand feet above, the crews felt disappointed. The "tallboys" did not make a splash of brilliant light like the blockbusters but showed only momentary red pin-points as they speared into the earth and exploded nearly a hundred feet deep. The little flashes they made were all round the markers but the crews turned for home with a feeling of anti-climax, and it was not till the recce Mosquito landed next morning with photographs that the impact of what they had done hit them. With one exception the fantastic craters were round the tunnel mouth, two of them in a line along the rails as though giant bites a hundred feet across and seventy feet deep had been torn out of the track bed.

But what really staggered everyone was the bomb that had fallen on the hill 60 yards from the tunnel mouth. No one ever found out whose bomb it was, which is a pity, because some bomb aimer would have received an instant decoration (though the credit should really go to Barnes Wallis). The hill rose steeply from the tunnel mouth, and under the spot where this bomb hit lay 70 feet of solid earth and chalk down to the tunnel. The bomb had bored straight through it into the tunnel itself and exploded there. Something like 10,000 tons of earth and chalk were blown sky-high and the mountain collapsed into the tunnel. It was one of the most startling direct hits of all time.

The panzer division did not get through. It was several days before dribs and drabs of them started to reach the invasion front on other transport, but by then it was too late for the decisive counter-attack they were supposed to have made. (The morning after the raid the Germans collected all the excavation gear in the district and slaved for weeks clearing the tunnel, filling in the craters and laying new rails. They just had it nicely finished when the Allies broke out of their bridgehead and took it over.)

And then, so soon after the invasion, the V1 "buzz-bombs" started to fall on London. The V2 rockets would follow soon. . . . Intelligence was sure of that.

CHAPTER XVI

SMASHING THE SECRET WEAPON

CHESHIRE was dragged out of sleep to find his batman tugging at his shoulder.

"Phone, sir."

He took up the phone and heard the Base Intelligence Officer's voice: "Can you please come over to the ops. room right away. It's urgent, sir."

He was there in ten minutes, and the intelligence officer greeted him with a few words that shook the last of the sleep out of him: "The secret weapon has started, sir. They're landing missiles on London and the invasion ports. Don't know how serious it is yet, but you're to stand by to take off as soon as the weather clears. This is your target," he passed over an aerial photograph, an enlargement that showed an enormous square concrete building. "We don't know how thick the concrete is," the intelligence officer was saying, "but as far as we can gather from agents over there it might be up to twenty feet thick . . . roof as well as the walls. It's near a place called Watten, just behind the Pas de Calais."

Air Commodore Sharp, the base commander, bustled in. "You know about these from the A.O.C.," he said. "I gather the rest of Bomber Command is cracking at the mobile sites, but they think the worst trouble will come from these four blockhouses, and your 'tallboys' are the only things with a hope of touching them. You'll have to go in daylight to see your aiming points properly and mark them with smoke bombs. We'll give you fighter cover."

Cochrane had a word with him over the phone a little later, brief and to the point: "We've got to knock these out somehow, and we'll have to go on until we do. Whitehall is all set for the evacuation of London and we don't know yet whether these things might wreck the invasion. You'll have to work hard."

To lay on a raid, plan it, brief the crews, bomb and fuel the aircraft took at least two hours. This time it was more difficult, because the "tallboys" needed special handling, but they did it inside two hours that morning. The crews were briefed and they all went down to the flights, pulled on their flying kit and waited. Over the Pas de Calais a sheet of ten-tenths stratus cloud stretched for miles at 2,000 feet, making it impossible to bomb. They could not have seen any aiming point from above, and they would have to bomb from at least 15,000 feet for penetration. The idea was to get near misses as much as direct hits. A direct hit might not pierce the concrete roof, but near misses would bore into the earth by the foundations and shake the structure with earthquakes. Wallis thought that a near miss up to 40 yards away would do more damage than a direct hit.

The crews stood by all day at the flights. It went on for three days like that till bed was only a memory. They lived down by the aeroplanes while the low cloud lingered over France and the buzz-bombs kept falling, ate cold food brought from the mess and tried to sleep curled up in blankets on the floors.

On the morning of the third day, exhausted, they were stood down and went off to bed, and in the early afternoon the clouds over France rolled away. From Group came the instant call ordering a "time on target" which gave them a bare ninety minutes to get airborne. By some sort of miracle the eighteen Lancasters, headed by two Mosquitoes, were climbing away from Woodhall on the scheduled minute.

Cheshire flew over Calais at 8,000 feet and searched the area for several minutes before he was able to pin-point the camouflaged mass of concrete in the ground haze. The earth for a mile around was torn up by the fruitless bombs of other raids, so that nothing stood out clearly. As he flew over it seventy guns opened up and black puffs stained the air all round him.

He felt reluctantly that there was only one thing to do: ten miles away he peeled off, held the nose steeply down and came in straight and fast on high power, so the engines were screaming in his ears and the plane shaking like a live thing. He let his smoke bombs go at 2,000 feet (as it was daylight the smoke would show more clearly than red flares), pulled steeply out of the hail of fire, marvellously untouched, looked back and saw no sign of smoke. The markers had failed to ignite.

Shannon dived the other Mosquito in the same way, and as he pulled up smoke puffed on the ground near the target. In the haze it seemed near enough, and there were no markers left anyway, so Cheshire called the Lancasters and saw them wheel in at 18,000 feet, open bomb doors and track stolidly through the flak. Fascinated, he saw the "tallboys" for the first time falling in daylight, the sun glinting off them as they streaked down, picking up speed till they were moving faster than sound, and then they vanished in a wisp of dust in the moment of impact. They had eleven-second delayed fuses and the seconds dragged till the ground burst in the shadow of the concrete and tens of thousands of tons of earth reared up in a climbing mushroom. Cheshire gaped, and beside him, dumbfounded, Kelly muttered, "God help the Jerries!" The target was hidden.

Recce photos later showed the bombs had circled Shannon's smoke markers, but also showed the markers had been about 70 yards wide. Some of the "tallboys" had fallen some 50 yards from the concrete target and, in the hopes that they had done the job, Cochrane sent 617 next day to Wizernes, where a huge concrete dome, 20 feet thick, lay on the edge of a chalk quarry, protecting rocket stores and launching tunnels that led out of the face of the quarry, pointing towards London.

The squadron reached the spot but found it hidden under cloud and brought their "tallboys" back. Cheshire landed with a new idea forming in his mind. If a Mosquito was better for marking than a Lancaster, then an even smaller and faster aircraft should be better still. He took his idea to Sharp, and the base commander said: "The American fighters have got the range you want. How about a Mustang or a P.38?" Cheshire said he thought that either would be ideal, and Sharp promised to try and get one.

Meantime Cheshire took 617 to Wizernes again but once more the cloud hid it. On the 24th they tried again and this time located the camouflaged dome dimly in the ground haze. Cheshire dived through brisk flak but his smoke bombs "hung up," so Fawke dived and laid his markers on the edge of the dome and the bombs fells spectacularly round the markers. Three of them exploded next to the tunnels in the side of the quarry, one sliced deep under the edge of the dome, and Dicky Willsher, who had just had his twentieth birthday, sent one right into the mouth of one of the tunnels. The face of the quarry seemed to burst open.

The flak got Edwards's plane on the run-up. A shell exploded in the port wing and the tanks caught fire. The others saw the Lancaster lose height slowly for a few seconds and then the nose dropped into a steep dive and she went over on her back. Two parachutes came out before she hit and the "tallboy" blew up. It was the first crew the squadron had lost for several weeks. Several men had been wounded in the air and a few aircraft written off, but for some weeks death had taken a holiday, the longest holiday it ever took in the squadron.

When he landed back at Woodhall, Cheshire found a Mustang waiting. Sharp's American friends had promptly said, "Sure," and an American pilot had flown one over. The pilot explained the cockpit to Cheshire, bade him a cheerful farewell and left him inspecting his new toy. It was only then he began to realise fully what he had taken on. He had never flown an American aircraft before; in fact, had not flown a single-engined aircraft since his early training days five years before. He had never flown a single-engined fighter at all, nor had he had to do his own navigation for years.

Cheshire decided that before he took it for a practice flip he would try and learn a little more about it, but those prudent hopes crashed in the morning when Cochrane ordered the squadron off for the Siracourt rocket site. They found then that the smoke markers would not fit in the racks under the Mustang's wings, and the armourers worked like furies rigging a makeshift wire contraption to hold the markers on. One of the navigators helped Cheshire work out his courses, and he wrote them on a piece of paper and strapped it to his knee. He took off in the Mustang half an hour early to get the feel of it, but did not try any practice landings; there was too much chance of breaking it on his first landing, and if he was going to do that he preferred it to be after the raid had been done.

It is unlikely that a pilot has ever before or since done an operation—particularly such a specialist one—on his first flight in a new type of plane. The change in his case from multi-engined to single-engined fighter makes the feat all the more remarkable. It bristled with difficulties. His timing had to be within thirty seconds over the target to co-ordinate with the bombers, and the Mustang cruised about 90 m.p.h. faster than the Lancasters. He could not very well work out changes of wind as well as map-read and fly. He had to be his own navigator, bomb aimer, gunner and wireless operator as well as learn to fly a new type well enough in an hour to be able to dive-bomb through thick flak.

From the start the Mustang delighted him and inside half an hour he felt he had the "feel" of it. She was lighter than the Mosquito and there was no comparison at all with a Lancaster. From 7,000 feet he spotted the concrete slab that protected the underground Siracourt rocket dump, and when the bombers reached the marshalling point he dived to 500 feet, revelling in the way the Mustang picked up speed, and put his smoke bombs within a few feet of the concrete. Someone put a "tallboy" through the middle of the slab, and it pierced 16 feet of ferro-concrete before it exploded. Another hit the western wall and blew it in, and another erupted deep under the rim of the slab.

Night had fallen when they got back from Siracourt, and

Cheshire's first Mustang landing had to be a night landing, which makes it about twice as difficult. He remembers little about it (in the same way that a man who bales out never remembers pulling the rip-cord) except that suddenly the little fighter was rolling smoothly on the runway, to his mild surprise and relief.

Grey cloud still hung over the Pas de Calais; it was forming over the North Sea and blowing over the land, and 617 stood by at dawn every day waiting for it to lift while the buzz-bombs fell on London. To the south the invasion was locked in the bridgehead, and even if they broke out the Seine still barred the way to the rocket sites. In London the nation's leaders (though not the unaware people) waited anxiously in case the mystery sites should start up. They guessed they must be nearly ready.

At last, on July 4, the weather cleared. Not a moment too soon. London was taking a beating. As the clouds rolled away over France 617 took off to hit back, target this time being the big store of rockets and buzz-bombs hidden in a cave at Creil, near Paris. It ran deep under a hill—at least 25 feet of chalk and clay over it—and the idea was both to collapse it and seal it up. Fawke went ahead in a Mosquito to get weather and wind information in advance. Cheshire flew his now beloved Mustang, and seventeen Lancasters carried the "tallboys".

Cheshire dived to 200 feet and aimed his markers so accurately that Fawke did not have to back up. Several "tallboys" then smashed through the cave roof with great ease; others collapsed the entrance and wrecked the railway that brought the rockets into the cave.

Next afternoon to Mimoyecques, where the Germans were sinking the fantastic gun barrels 500 feet into the ground to fire 600 tons of explosive a day on London. War Cabinet still did not know this; they only knew it was one of Hitler's secret-weapon sites. From above it was nearly invisible, a

30 by 20 yards square of camouflaged concrete shielding the gun tunnels beneath.

An hour before dusk Cheshire, in the Mustang, found the spot in the chalk hills behind Calais, dived and lobbed his markers on it. When the "tallboys" came down he saw one direct hit, and four were "very near misses," which were probably more effective.

A message summoning him to Cochrane met him when he landed and he drove straight over to Group. Cochrane said when he walked in: "I've been looking at the records and I see you've done a hundred trips now. That's enough; it's time you had a rest. I've got hold of Tait to take over." Cheshire opened his mouth to argue and Cochrane said, "It's no use arguing. . . . Sorry, but there it is. A hundred is a good number to stop at." He went on and thanked him, quietly and with no flowery nonsense, and dropped another bombshell: "Shannon, Munro and McCarthy will come off too. They've been going continuously for about two years and it's time they had a rest as well."

There were, as Cheshire expected, protests from Shannon, Munro and McCarthy, but from that moment they were changed men, gayer, but in a less violent way, and only then he realised that the strain had been telling on his three durable flight commanders.

They had earned a rest; all of them had D.S.Os., D.F.Cs. and Bars. The squadron gave them a send-off at which one or two (prodded perhaps by alcohol) were near tears, but before the hangovers had subsided Wing Commander Willie Tait had arrived to take over. He put Fawke up to flight commander and brought two veteran pilots, Cockshott and Iveson, as his other lieutenants. Tait was a Welshman, belonging to no recognisable type but with a unique Celtic streak of his own. Smoothly brown-skinned and slim, with straight black hair, he had his own brand of introspection and dry wit. He was twenty-six, had two D.S.Os. and a D.F.C.

The cloud was back over France, so that for ten days there was no bombing; a lucky reprieve for the rocket sites, but at least it gave the squadron a chance to settle down under the new leaders, and Tait a chance to learn the marking technique in the Mustang.

On July 17 Met. reported the clouds rolling away, and a couple of hours later 617 was on the way to Wizernes. For this, his first marking effort, Tait flew one of the Mosquitoes with Danny Walker as navigator. Thick haze lay over the ground and they circled a long time in the flak before they could faintly pick up the great blockhouse merging with the torn earth. Tait dived from 7,000 to 500 feet before he let his smoke marker go accurately, and Fawke backed up. A few minutes later both Knights and Kearns got direct hits with "tallboys", and several more "tallboys" sent up awe-inspiring eruptions 40 to 50 yards away, more or less where Wallis preferred them.

More days of waiting for the weather, and on the 20th they went back to Wizernes. Tait, flying the Mustang for the first time on business, found wisps of broken cloud drifting over the area and thick haze on the ground. A lot of flak was coming up; he dived through it and lobbed his smoke markers, pulled steeply up to 4,000 feet, looked down and could only just see the smoke drifts. Obviously the bombers, miles back at 18,000 feet, would never see it, and so he did an unheard-of thing . . . called up the bombers and said, "Try and aim at me," then dived into the bursting flak directly over the blockhouse and circled it at 1,000 feet, hoping the glinting of his wings would draw the eyes of the bomb aimers to the spot.

The Mustang shook in the shell blasts, and little holes were suddenly appearing in the wings and fuselage as machine-gun bullets and shrapnel punched through. Two bullets went through the petrol tank (which was self-sealing) and just missed the glycol coolant tank (which was not), and even then the bomb aimers did not see him.

They called up on their bombing runs and said they could

not identify a thing, and Tait at last swung away out of the flak, an extremely lucky young man to be still airborne and personally unpunctured. The squadron turned and brought their "tallboys" back home.

They waited five more days for the cloud to clear and on the 25th went to Watten, Tait again in the Mustang. Murderous flak came spitting up all round the blockhouse, but this time, for the first time in weeks, there was neither haze nor cloud and in the crystal-clear air the target stood out so clearly that the bomb aimers reported they could see it from miles back, and Tait did not have to mark.

They had half-hour delay fuses on the "tallboys" that day, so they saw no explosions, but as the bombs sliced into the earth puffs of dust shot into the air from the shadow of the blockhouses.

Fawke lingered half an hour near the spot with a camera in his Mosquito and brought back beautiful photographs of the explosions . . . five direct hits and half a dozen very *very* near misses. Three aircraft were badly hit by flak and one gunner died, his throat cut by flak.

Again they waited for the weather and on July 31 flew to deal with a flying-bomb storage dump in a railway tunnel near Rilly La Montagne. They caved in each entrance to the tunnel with their uncanny accuracy. They lost another crew that day.

The liberating armies burst out and reached the Pas de Calais area and, as it happened, there was nothing for them to do about the rocket sites except stare in wonder. 617 had destroyed them.

At Watten they found that "tallboys" had smashed the roof and wrecked the building inside so badly that the Germans had abandoned it.

The great rocket site at Wizernes was reduced to rubble. The 10,000-ton dome on top was knocked off its foundations and the launching tunnels below had caved in.

At Creil they found that the deep limestone caves which were to have protected their rockets and buzz-bombs had collapsed for hundreds of yards and buried them instead.

A "tallboy" had gone right through the 16-foot concrete roof at Siracourt site, exploded beneath it and wrecked it.

Most spectacular was the wreckage at Mimoyecques, where the fabulous guns of V3 were to have fired on London. One "tallboy" had ripped a corner off the 20-foot thick concrete roof and completely blocked the left-hand gun shaft. A near miss had collapsed the right-hand shaft and shaken the remaining shaft out of plumb. Five hundred feet down when the bombers came, 300 workers had been sheltering in what they must have thought was complete safety. They are still there, entombed.

Churchill sent Wallis over to France, to see what his "tallboys" had done, with an eye to what they might do in the future. When he flew home Harris silently showed him photographs of the workmen swarming over the concrete U-boat pens at Hamburg, Bremen and Ijmuiden. They were enormous pens, some of them 300 feet square and 70 feet high. It was obvious that they were being further strengthened. Agents' reports confirmed this.

"Looks as though we're going to have some more substantial targets," Harris said. "After what you've seen of the rocket sites, do you think a 'tallboy' could cope with these?"

"I think one or two 'tallboys' broke up on the concrete," Wallis said. "If we're going to have something still bigger to deal with, I think we should throw something bigger at them." He added artlessly, "Something like a ten-tonner. I've been suggesting a ten-tonner for some time now, and I believe the Lancaster has developed enough to carry it into Germany."

Harris looked at him. He said after a while, "Mr. Wallis, I said once you could sell me a pink elephant. I think perhaps this time you might at last sell your ten-tonner."

That was a *very* satisfying day in Wallis's life.

CHAPTER XVII

VICTORIA CROSS

6 1 7 WAS a delighted squadron; not because of the coming 10-ton bomb (they were not told about that yet) but because Leonard Cheshire had just been awarded the V.C. It was the second V.C. to the credit of the newest squadron in the R.A.F., and one of the most remarkable V.Cs. ever awarded.

The citation specified no one act of superb gallantry but listed some of the things he had done: the time a shell had burst inside his aircraft and he had continued on to the target, his volunteering for a second tour as soon as he had finished his first, his third tour, and then his insistence on dropping rank to do a fourth in a "suicide squadron". There was a piece on his part in the Munich raid, when he cruised through the flak over the roof-tops, and it noted that he had done a hundred raids. A V.C. is often won in a moment of exalted heroism, but there can be no tougher way of winning it than by four years of persistent bravery.

617 had lost its priority targets now and Cochrane was busy finding new ones of sufficient importance and diminutiveness to merit the "tallboys" and 617's specialist attention. Tait had been completely accepted by the squadron. An *élite* corps, they had regarded him a little aloofly (after Cheshire and Martin) until he had gone down to circle Wizernes in his Mustang as a personal aiming point for the bombs as well as the flak; then they went so far as to chide him with fond concern for sticking his neck out so imprudently.

Wallis's new 10-tonner was coming along as fast as possible. but that was not very fast because it was a far more complicated job, even, than the "tallboy". Freeman had christened it with the code name of "Grand Slam" and delivery date for the first one was roughly February, 1945. Meantime the Americans were starting to produce "tallboys" and were evolving a new (and very efficient) method of making "grand slams".

It might be said that the fate of the battleship was finally sealed in the bath of Air Vice-Marshal the Honourable Ralph Cochrane. In his waking moments work was rarely absent from his mind; he had been thinking of the *Tirpitz* for a long time, and it was in his bath one morning that he finally made up his mind to get permission for 617 to sink her. He climbed out, dried, dressed and flew down to see Harris, and Harris said yes.

Tirpitz was still in Alten Fiord, in the Arctic Circle, by the northern tip of Norway. Merely lying inside her girdle of torpedo nets she forced the Allies to divert three battleships, badly needed elsewhere, to guard the Russia convoys. The Allies had been trying to "get" her for over two years. First a Russian submarine damaged her; then British midget submarines put her out of action for six months. Next the Fleet Air Arm hit her, but now she was ready for sea again.

Cochrane flew to Woodhall. "Tait," he said (typical of the man), "you're going to sink the *Tirpitz*." For a while they discussed ways and means. One problem, Cochrane warned, would be the smoke screen round the ship. The Germans had run a pipeline round the shores of the narrow fiord and could pour out smoke by turning a tap. Also there were scores of smoke pots round the ship, and they could smother the fiord under smoke in eight minutes. There would be no time to waste manœuvring for a bomb run. Tait went over to the mess to have a glass of beer and think about it.

He spread maps on his office floor and measured the distance there and back. It was formidable: something like 3,000 miles . . . probably beyond range. He loaded three Lancasters with bombs and full petrol and sent off three of the youngest crews (because the maximum range is what the least experienced can do) to fly round England a distance equal to the distance to the target. He sent another plane with half petrol to fly similarly, representing the distance back with a lighter load. When they landed he measured the petrol they had used, and the two ends of the string did not meet. He reported to Cochrane that the *Tirpitz* was just outside their range.

Two days later Cochrane flew over and said, "You can do it from Russia." He put a finger on the map. . . . "Here. Yagodnik." Yagodnik was a Russian airfield on an island in the Dvina River, about twenty miles from Archangel . . . only 600 miles from Alten Fiord. "Fly to Yagodnik from northern Scotland with your bombs," Cochrane said. "Refuel there, do the job, return to Yagodnik to refuel again and come home."

He said there were enough "tallboys" now to send 9 Squadron with them. 9 Squadron could not use the S.A.B.S. but had become nearly as accurate with the Mark XIV bomb sight. Two Liberators would carry ground crews and spares.

The planners worked fast and three days later, on a good weather report, the squadron (carrying their "tallboys") flew to Lossiemouth, refuelled and in bright sunshine on September 10 took off heavily on the long haul to Russia.

Rain poured on Yagodnik, and for three days they waited for it to lift. Friendly Russians tried hard to amuse them, but outside the huts lay a sea of mud and the crews relaxed indoors, chasing bugs and eating sour black bread, borscht and half-cooked bacon . . . when the last of the breakfasters rose the head of the lunch queue sat down.

On September 15 the sun crawled out of the horizon low to the south and shone in a clear sky. The crews were out in their aircraft, running up the engines hopefully, when the weather plane darted over the airfield like a blue kingfisher and landed with the report that the sky over Alten Fiord was clear. Minutes later twenty-eight Lancasters of the two squadrons were lifting off the bumpy grass and turning west. Tait flew slowly, the rest of his squadron picking up station behind till they were in their gaggle low over the White Sea, and on strict radio silence to delay detection. Grey water close below muffled the thunder of the engines till they crossed the barren shore of Lapland and the echoes came up from the ice-worn rocks. The land was lifeless but for odd stunted trees; it rose a little and the aircraft lifted their noses gently over the contours.

Tait had an engine running rough, shaking the plane like a rolling-mill, but he headed on worrying about having enough power for the bombing climb. Ninety miles from Alten Fiord the mountains reared ahead and, on full throttle and revs., Tait's rough engine cleared and he climbed easily over the last ridge. They were dead on track.

Alten Fiord lay quietly in the sun like a map; they raced for it at 11,000 feet to beat the smoke screen, but as they picked out the black shape at her anchorage under the cliff, white plumes started vomiting out of the smoke pots and streaming across the water.

The bombers were quivering on full power five minutes from bombing point as the white veils started wreathing her. There must have been a hundred pots pouring smoke. Flak was firing from the heights now; the gaggle ran steadily through the black puffs, and then the *Tirpitz*'s guns opened up. Two minutes from release point the drifting veils were fast smothering her. Daniels, in the nose of Tait's aircraft, took a long bead and called, "Bomb sight on!"

The black hull finally vanished in its shroud but the masttops stood clear a few seconds later, and then they too were gone. Daniels tried to hold his graticule on the spot but found no mark in the drifting smoke and guessed as the seconds dragged that he must be wandering off. The Lancaster leapt as the bomb clattered away and Tait swung the wheel hard over, swerving out of the flak.

Behind him the others had all lost their mark in that agonising last minute. Howard, Watts and Sanders bombed on dim gun flashes through the smoke. Kell and Knilans bombed on the spot last seen, and the others, in frustration, did not bomb at all. Pale flickers in the smoke showed bombs exploding, and after one of them a plume of black smoke spurted through the whiteness. Tait felt a moment of hope but judged it was only a "tallboy" striking the shore. Some of the Lancasters swung back through the flak for a second run, but the screen was thicker than ever and they turned for base.

It was the nearness to success that hurt Cochrane most. He said wryly, "Another minute's sight and you'd have got her. I was afraid those smoke pots might balk you." He did not tell Tait at the time but he had no intention of leaving the *Tirpitz* in peace.

Recce aircraft reported the *Tirpitz* was missing from Alten Fiord and there was a great "flap" (particularly among the nautical people) till a message came through from a Mr. Egil Lindberg. Lindberg was a Norwegian who operated a secret transmitter from a room above the morgue in Tromso. The *Tirpitz* had arrived in Tromso, he reported, with a great hole in her for'd deck. She had been hit by a very heavy bomb (Daniels' "tallboy" *had* hit the ship. He was probably the most "hawk-eyed" bomb aimer of the war). Lindberg thought the *Tirpitz* had come to Tromso because the repair facilities were better there. Cochrane got the news and did not care a hoot about the repair facilities. The important thing to him was that Tromso was 200 miles south of Alten Fiord—it shortened the return trip by 400 miles . . . and that put the *Tirpitz* just within range of Lossiemouth.

A new consideration interrupted Cochrane's *Tirpitz* plans. The right flank of the American dash across France into Germany had been halted at the Belfort Gap; ahead the Rhine barred the way into Germany, and on the Rhine by the Swiss frontier lay the Kembs Dam. It was obvious that when the Americans stormed the river the Germans would blow up the flood-gates, releasing a massive head of water that would sweep the assault forces to destruction in mid-river or isolate those who got across. There was only one way out—smash the flood-gates first, let the water spend itself and then drive at the river.

Cochrane decided that a "tallboy" dropped low over the water just short of the flood-gates would slide cleanly into the water till it hit a gate and stick in the concrete. They would give it a delayed fuse so the low-flying bombers would not be blown up as well.

It would have to be done very accurately; that meant doing it in full daylight, and the dam was circled with guns. The bombers would have to fly very low, straight and level, and run the gauntlet. No question as to who should do it!

Cochrane planned it craftily. They would split in two formations; one would come in and bomb from the west at 8,000 feet, drawing the flak; and in the precise moment their bombs were hitting, six Lancasters would sneak in low from the east for the real assault. At the same instant a Mustang squadron would dive on the flak-pits with guns and rockets so the flak might not notice the low-level force, at least till the bombs were gone. It was going to need split-second timing, and 617 practised every day for a week till their final rehearsal over Wainfleet went perfectly. Tait was insisting on leading the low-level force.

They all took off into light haze and ran into a pall of cloud over Manston, where they were to meet the fighters. Tait called the fighter leader and told him they were overhead. It was clear over France. They skirted the Swiss frontier, slid past Basle on the right and turned down the river, opening bomb doors. Three miles ahead Tait saw flashes round the low parapet of the Kembs, but the guns were aiming high at Fawke's formation. Great flashes and columns of spray rushed up round the dam; the timing of the high-force bombs was perfect. Tait's aeroplane was rock-steady on course and no word was spoken, except once, a terse "O.K." from Daniels. They were committed to it now, sliding over the smooth water with taut nerves and dry mouths. Tait saw Mustangs diving out of the sun over the dam and dared to hope the flak would not see him, but abruptly the white-hot balls came darting at them. He felt the plane jump as the bomb slid away, slammed the throttles on, did not see the bomb knife cleanly into the water 10 yards from the right-hand sluice-gate, but heard the vibrant rattle as the rear gunner opened up and they hurtled over the dam.

Behind him Castagnola's plane lurched in Tait's slipstream and threw the bomb wide. Tait hauled hard over to the right for the shelter of the hills, climbing on full power, engines blaring in fine pitch as they dragged her up. He turned abeam and saw a Lancaster rocking over the dam on fire, flame and smoke streaming in her wake. She dropped a wing and plunged into the river bank, rolling over in a ball of fire. When it is quick it is a good way to die.

Tait heard a voice in his earphones—Howard's, he thought —saying, "Had a hang-up. Going round again." Howard, of the noble family, was rather a formal boy, but brave. Perhaps foolhardy. This time the gunners were wary, not distracted. Howard came alone down the river and all the guns saw him. They got him a long way back and he blew up in mid-air with the bomb on board.

The surviving bombers turned for home; in five minutes the sound of their engines had died away and the dam lay quietly in the sun as though nothing had happened, except for the two columns of greasy smoke pouring from the spots where Howard and Wyness and their crews had died.

There had been half-hour delay fuses on the low-force "tallboys". Twenty minutes after the raid a Mosquito droned high over the dam and circled it, the pilot watching till he saw the water beside the right-hand sluice-gate burst and mushroom into the air. A massive torrent plunged through the gate, and in twenty-four hours the banked headwaters of the Rhine had dropped so much that barges far into Switzerland grounded on the mud.

The next days were a fever of activity getting ready for the *Tirpitz*. With tests and graphs Tait worked it out that from Lossiemouth they could just reach the *Tirpitz* in Tromso with a bare—a very bare—safety margin in case of adverse winds.

In October and November a prevailing westerly blows continuous stratus cloud from the sea over Tromso . . . except for perhaps three days a month, when the wind briefly changes to the east and the sky is clear for a few hours. They would have to be in position at Lossiemouth to take off when one of these clear periods existed, and hope it would last till they got there. But neither Harris nor Cochrane could let them stay at Lossiemouth indefinitely "on spec". They needed them down south in case of emergency targets. The only way was for the squadron to fly to Lossiemouth when a break seemed possible.

The word came on October 28, and thirty-six Lancasters of 617 and 9 Squadrons flew north to a bleak field near Lossiemouth. At midnight a Mosquito over Tromso radioed that the wind was veering to the east, and in drizzling rain, at the deathly hour of 1 a.m., the overburdened Lancasters took off.

They flew low as usual, in sight of the caps on the dark water; hours later crossed the Norwegian coast and turned inland towards Sweden to keep the mountains between them and the Tromso radar. They wheeled left in a long climb, topped the ridges and saw Tromso Fiord and the ship . . . and saw in the same moment, moving in from the sea, towering drifts of cloud. The wind had changed.

It was a race again, like those sickening moments over Alten Fiord, but this time the white screens were higher and thicker. At 230 m.p.h. the bombers charged towards the ship and the cloud. A minute from release point they still saw the ship, but with thirty seconds to go the cloud slid between them.

They couldn't dive under it to bomb; lower down the "tallboys" would not have penetrated the armoured decks. Daniels tried to keep his bomb sight on the spot where he last saw the ship. Flak was bursting through the cloud among them now. Daniels called "Bomb gone!" and Tait dived into the cloud to try and see where it fell. Fawke, Iveson, Knights and one or two more bombed on vague glimpses and dived too. Others swung away to try another run. Through gaps in the cloud at about 13,000 feet Tait saw flashes as bombs exploded in the water round the ship. One or two others said they thought they saw a direct hit or near miss.

Carey's Lancaster had been hit by flak on the first run; the starboard outer engine stopped and petrol streamed out of a riven tank, luckily without catching fire. He turned back on three engines for another run and the cloud foiled him. He tried again and again, ploughing steadfastly through the flak till, on the sixth run, an almost desperate bomb aimer let his "tallboy" go with faint hope.

Tait had ordered everyone to dive to 1,000 feet to pick up speed and steer for home. As Carey screamed down he passed over a small island: a single gun on it pumped a shell into another engine, which died instantly; petrol was streaming out of another burst tank (miraculously no fire again), and then the hydraulics burst and the bomb doors and under-carriage flopped down. The two good engines on full power just held her in the air against the drag; the engineer thumbed his gauges, scribbed a few calculations and said, "Sorry, Skip. Not enough gas to get home."

From the rear turret came a protesting, grimly flippant voice: "This can't happen to me." Witherick was flying with Carey this time. He had a habit of switching crews.

"Can't it?" said Carey. "You watch!"

He turned the winged plane towards the land and, staggering through the air a few hundred feet up, they threaded through a mountain pass and slowly crossed the barren country. Half an hour later the navigator said they were over Sweden. The two engines were dangerously hot and Carey crash-landed in a bog near Porjus. The Lancaster tilted frighteningly on her nose, poised a moment and settled back, and they climbed out.

The rest of the squadron landed at Lossiemouth and heard that a recce plane radioed that the *Tirpitz* was untouched. They flew down to Woodhall, where Tait found a message from Cochrane: "Congratulations on your splendid flight and perseverance. The luck won't always favour the *Tirpitz*. One day you'll get her."

CHAPTER XVIII

THE NAKED BATTLESHIP

A NEW complication jolted Cochrane. Intelligence reported that twenty to thirty German fighters had moved in to Bardufoss airfield, thirty miles from Tromso. No doubting why! Two strong attacks had been made on the *Tirpitz*; the Germans would give the next one a lethal reception. Cochrane found himself in the old position of the commander forced to stay at his desk and decide whether to send his men into an ambush. For all his coldness there was a personal factor this time that he tried to eliminate. 617 never knew (and would never have guessed) that they were the apple of his eye; he had a respect for them amounting to affection.

But it was an operational war. That was the clinching factor. He decided they would have to go if the cloud let them.

Next day the weather was improving. Tait was playing football with his crews on the airfield, surrounded by the circle of silent cloaked Lancasters, when he was summoned to the operations room, and there, still in striped jersey and studded boots, he got his orders. In a few hours they were flying up to Northern Scotland.

Some time after midnight the weather Mosquito, sliding through darkness on the way back from Tromso, reported fog in the fiords and cloud half-way up Norway. There was a possibility Tromso might be clear by dawn, but there were distinct icing conditions (a real bogy for heavy-laden aircraft). It was not encouraging. Tait discussed it with the Met. men, and at the end he said, "All right. We'll give it a go."

They flew slowly to save petrol, flame floats bobbing on the

water in their wake as they checked for drift. Tait had slipped
in the automatic pilot and tried to doze, as he always did on out-
ward trips over water; he believed in taking sleep when he
could get it, but seldom got it.

The sky was paling in the east as they reached the Norwegian
coast, turned right, climbed over the mountains and dipped
into the inland valleys. The sun lifted over the horizon and
the valleys lay soft under snow, flecked with bare rocks. Snow
crests surrounded them, tops laced with pink like vast wedding
cakes, except to the south, where the sun splintered on the ice-
peaks and sparkled with the colours of the spectrum like a
diamond necklace, radiantly lovely. Fog-filled lakes passed
slowly below but there was no cloud. Rendezvous was a narrow lake cradled between steep hills a hundred miles south-
east of Tromso, and Tait flew slowly towards it, saw no water
but recognised it as a long pool of fog in the trough and over it
saw aircraft circling like black flies.

He flew across it firing Véry lights to draw them, and they
turned in behind and started the climb towards Tromso.
That was the moment the radar picked them up, and within
a minute the fighter operations room at Bardufoss knew that
enemy bombers were closing on the *Tirpitz*. At 14,000 feet
the bombers were all at battle stations. One last mountain
shouldered up, and as they lifted over the peak it lowered like a
screen and there again, folded in the cliffs, lay Tromso Fiord
and the black ship, squat in the distance, like a spider in her
web of torpedo nets. It was like looking down from the
"gods" on a Wagnerian stage, a beetle in green water cupped
in the snowy hills, all coral and flame. There was no cloud.
And no smoke screen. *Tirpitz* lay naked to the bomb sights.

Even the air was still. On the flanks of the gaggle Tait saw
the front rank riding steadily. They seemed suspended;
motionless but for the sublime hills falling slowly behind, immaculate and glowing with the beauty of sunrise and the in-
difference of a million years to the ugliness of the intrusion. So
must many an Arctic coast burn unseen.

Far below the basin seemed to sleep in the shadow, but *Tirpitz* broke the spell with a salvo, sparkling from stem to stern with flashes as billows of smoke from the guns wreathed her and drifted up. Her captain had just radioed urgently to Bardufoss to hurry the fighters.

Tait opened the bomb doors and slid the pitch levers up to high revs.; the engines bellowed and the exhausts glowed even in that cold light. Black puffs stained the sky among the gaggle as the flak reached them, and then the guns round the fiord opened fire. Tait watched anxiously for the smoke pots, but the smoke never came (the pots were there all right, just brought down from Alten, but the Germans had not yet primed them). The bomb sight was on and the ship drawing nearer while the gunners in the rear turrets watched the ridges anxiously for the first fighters. It was all up to the rear gunners when the fighters came; there were no mid-upper gunners.

Now it was water, far below, sliding under the nose. Tait felt his hands on the wheel were clammy, and Daniels' breathing rasped over the intercom. The bomber was unswerving, shaking in the engines' thunder, and out of the cockpit Tait could see the bomb doors quivering as the air-flow battered at them. The red light came on—ten seconds to go . . . seconds that dragged till "D Dog" leapt as the grips snapped back and the bomb lurched away. Tait hauled hard over to the left and on either side saw others of the front rank doing likewise.

One by one the gaggle wheeled as the bombs went. They watched, wordless, through the perspex for thirty seconds till a great yellow flash burst on the battleship's foredeck. From 14,000 feet they saw her tremble. Another bomb hit the shore; two more in close succession hit the ship, one on the starboard side, by the bridge, and another abaft the funnel. Another one split the sea 5 feet from her bows, and then the smoke pall covered her and only dimly through it they saw the other bursts all inside the crinoline of nets.

One constant glare shone through the smoke. She was burning. There came another flash and a plume of steam jetted 500 feet into the air through the smoke as a magazine went up.

Three minutes later 9 Squadron bombed the dark shroud over her, and then the black flies crawling in the sky turned south-west and curved down towards the sea, picking up speed for the run home. They never saw a fighter. The last thing they saw as the smoke lifted was the *Tirpitz* starting to list.

The cloud they had feared closed in on the long slog home, and Tait was driving blindly through it when his artificial horizon collapsed in a mess of ball bearings and mechanism. After eleven hours in the air his eyes felt like hot coals as he focused rigidly on the other instruments; then the aerial iced up and they could not get a homing for a long time, and when they did it was a diversion. Lossiemouth was cloaked in rain, and Tait turned east and found a small Coastal Command field, where he touched down smoothly.

At the control tower a young pilot officer asked if they had been on a cross-country, and Tait primly pursed his mouth, looked in aloof shyness at the ground and said, "Yes".

They drove over to Lossiemouth, where they met the rest of the squadron, and were drinking in the bar when the recce plane radioed that *Tirpitz* was upside down in Tromso Fiord, her bottom humped over the water like a stranded whale.

It was not till after the war they found it had all been unnecessary. The bomb Tait and Daniels had dropped six weeks earlier at Alten Fiord had damaged *Tirpitz* beyond repair.

CHAPTER XIX

BACK FROM THE DEAD

AFTER the excitement of the *Tirpitz* came anti-climax. Unbroken cloud lay over Europe for weeks, making high precision bombing impossible. 617 stood by constantly, were briefed hopefully a dozen times and then the cancellations came. Once they got into the air but were recalled.

Carey, Witherick and company arrived back, gloating over their taste of peacetime flesh-pots in Sweden but furious at missing the end of the *Tirpitz*. "You might have waited for us, sir," Witherick said aggrievedly to Tait. "You *know* I always come back."

Increasing sea losses testified to the fact that Germany's fleet of "schnorkel" U-boats was increasing. For all the main force bombing, the U-boats found shelter in the massive concrete pens and Cochrane switched 617 on to them. They battered the pens at Ijmuiden (the port of Amsterdam) with six direct hits.

Cochrane decided that Tait had done enough. Tait had four D.S.Os. now and two D.F.Cs.—a record—and Cochrane did not want him to strain his luck too far. Shopping round for a new commander, he found no one with all the qualities he wanted till an air commodore heard the position was vacant and asked to be dropped in rank and given the job. This was Johnnie Fauquier, a Canadian, and a tough one, a thick-set, ex-bush pilot. Ten years older than most of them, he was as forceful as a steam-roller. Feeling that the war was almost over, the crews had been in a mood to relax and were scandalised when Fauquier got them out of bed in the frosty early mornings for P.T. Storms were sweeping over Europe and

the runways were snowed up, so there was no flying. Fauquier
gave them lectures instead, and then made them shovel snow
off the runways.

More days waiting for weather; more briefings, more cancellations, till January 12, when they went to Bergen, in Norway,
on the campaign against U-boats. For the first time Fauquier
flew a Mosquito to direct them and for the first time in months
German fighters fell on them like a swarm of hornets. They
got Pryor on their first strike and he went straight into the sea.
Three of them lunged at Nicky Ross on the flank of the gaggle.
Watts, next to him, saw the tracer flicking into the Lancaster
and lumps flying off her. He wheeled to help him, but Ross
was going down, slewing into a spiral with three engines
smashed. Near the water he seemed to recover; the spiral
stopped, the mad dive eased and the plane had almost flattened
out when it abruptly vanished in a sheet of spray. The rest
took vengeance. Someone put a "tallboy" squarely on the
stern of a large ship and in two minutes she had blown up,
rolled over and sunk. The rest got several direct hits on the
pens.

Next morning Chiefy Powell was sadly typing out the
casualty report on Nicky Ross (who had been on the squadron
nearly a year—longer than any other pilot) when the door
swung open and in walked Ross himself.

Powell gaped.

"Wotcher, Chiefy," quoth the ghost. "Home again!"

"Good God, sir! Where've you come from?"

"Air sea rescue picked us up. Cold in that dinghy." He
sat on a corner of the desk and rattled on amiably about the
details.

After some splutters Powell found speech. "D'you know
what I was doing when you walked in, sir? Typing your
death notice!"

"Ar, hold it for a while, Chiefy," said the cheerful Ross.
"You're a bit premature."

Meantime the first "grand slam" was nearly ready. Like

the "tallboy", its tail had offset aero-dynamic fins to make it spin so fast in falling that the gyroscopic effect would stop it toppling as it shuddered through the sonic barrier. When the tail was put on "grand slam" would be 25 feet 6 inches long. At its thickest part it was 3 feet 10 inches in diameter, and the finished bomb was to weigh just over 22,000 lb.

The German fighter force was nearly spent now, making it possible for 617's inadequately armed Lancasters to penetrate deeper and deeper against the enemy by day. They carried on with "tallboys" against the U-boat pens until Eisenhower asked the Air Forces for an all-out assault on German communications. The vulnerable points were the railway bridges, and most vital of these was the Bielefeld Viaduct, not far from Bremen, main link between the Wehrmacht defending the arsenal of the Ruhr and the great centres of north-west Germany. The idea was to starve the front of men and materials and split the country into "islands" that could be taken one by one.

Three thousand tons of bombs had already been aimed at the Bielefeld Viaduct; the earth for a mile around it was torn into overlapping craters, but the 75-foot arches of the viaduct still firmly bridged the marshes for the trains running south. The light-case bombs of the main bomber forces were not powerful enough to do more than chip it. Cochrane turned 617 on to it, and so began the battle of Bielefeld.

They took off with their "tallboys" one morning, but found the viaduct under ten-tenths cloud and brought them back. Next day they tried once more but again found unbroken cloud. Days later the cloud had cleared; they flew back to Bielefeld, found it reasonably clear and a few minutes later the viaduct was hidden under smoke as the "tallboys" crashed round it. Half an hour later, when the smoke lifted, a recce aircraft found the viaduct still there. "Tallboy" craters lay in its shadow, but the viaduct was no round target like a bull's-eye or a U-boat pen. From 18,000 feet it was almost indistinguishably threadlike.   It was like trying to stick a dart in a pencil line.

They waited on the weather and tried again a few days later, but once more found it under cloud. Doggedly they went back a fifth time and turned away in fuming frustration once more. There seemed to be something diabolical about the persistence of the cloud that shielded it.

That night two heavy trailers rolled round the perimeter track to the bomb dump carrying the first two "grand slams". In the morning armourers trollied them out and slowly winched them up into Fauquier's and Calder's Lancasters, specially modified in readiness for this day. They had the most powerful Merlin engines, the fuselages, undercarriages and main beams of the bomb bays had been strengthened and the bomb doors taken off (they could not have closed round the great girth of "Grand Slam").

"Grand Slam" had never been tested. There had not been time. Only one other "grand slam" existed, and that very morning a Lancaster was going to drop it over the range in the New Forest. Group was waiting for that, and also for the cloud to clear.

Just before noon Met. reported the cloud over Germany rolling away. As Fauquier was briefing his crews a phone message reached Group from the New Forest: "The beast went off all right!"

CHAPTER XX

"GRAND SLAM"

AT one o'clock 617's engines were bursting into life round the field. Fauquier was running up his engines, testing his magnetos, when there was a crash from the starboard inner and the propeller jerked to a grinding halt as it seized. Fauquier, muttering with frustration, knew the aircraft would never get off the ground on three engines. There was only one thing to do . . . borrow Calder's aircraft. The fact that he might then be shot down instead of Calder never even occurred to him, and would not have worried him if it had. He scuttled out of his plane and went haring across the field.

Calder saw the running figure, shouting and waving hands in urgent signals, guessed what had happened and cracked his throttles open. The Lancaster lurched forward and, with the small figure sprinting despairingly in the rear, rolled thunderously down the runway, picking up speed till it lifted heavily over the far fence on the way to drop the world's biggest bomb.

The "tallboy"-armed gaggle fell in behind, watching Calder's wings in wonder and alarm. On the ground a Lancaster has no perceptible dihedral, the wings spread in a flat, straight line, but Calder's wings now were a graceful arc, curving up at the tips as they took the strain of the 10-tonner. Those underneath could see the great missile hanging in the bomb bays where the bomb doors used to be.

The sky was clear of cloud; they skirted the flak at Bremen and ten minutes later picked up the line of the viaduct threading across the marshes. Calder headed in, the laden bomber thrusting smoothly through the bumps till Calder felt her bound up as the "grand slam" slipped away from the grips.

Wheeling away, they watched it drop like a silver shark, slowly starting to spin as its nose dipped lower and it picked up speed, lunging towards the viaduct. It fell for some thirty-five seconds and from far above the sharpest eyes picked up the squirt of mud as it speared into the marsh 30 yards from the foot of one of the arches.

Eleven seconds later the marsh seemed to split and a vast core of mud and smoke vomited up, blotting out 500 feet of the viaduct. In the next seconds "tallboy" explosions erupted along both sides of the viaduct. Calder peeled off to try and see what had happened; slowly the mud settled, the wind wafted the smoke away, and as the target appeared through the veils Calder saw that the viaduct looked like a Roman ruin. Seven massive arches over a hundred yards were missing.

He could see almost no collapsed masonry underneath and thought for a moment that the bomb had blasted the arches into dust, but could not believe that possible.

Later they found that the one "grand slam" had completely vindicated Barnes Wallis's theory that a near miss could be more effective than a direct hit. It had penetrated about a hundred feet, and the shock wave had shivered the arches to cracking point; the explosion had produced a near "camouflet", blasting an enormous subterranean cavity underneath, and, robbed of their foundation in the mud, the weakened arches had collapsed into the abyss. It was the perfect trapdoor effect, the "hangman's drop" that Wallis had planned in 1939.

In the next few days trailers delivered several more "grand slams" to the bomb dump, and on March 19 Fauquier got his delayed chance to drop one. The target was in historic territory for 617, the Arnsberg Bridge, a long masonry viaduct a few miles north of the Moehne Dam. Five Lancasters carried "grand slams", and the other fourteen had "tallboys". The first bomb was a direct hit on the viaduct, and the rest, including Fauquier's "grand slam", went down into the centre of the smoke that gushed up. When the smoke lifted, the central spans were a pile of rubble in the river bed.

Two days later they went to the Arbergen Bridge, near Bremen. Flak got a direct hit on Gumbley's aircraft on the run-up and he went straight down in flames. Price had to swerve out of the way of the falling aircraft, marring his bombing run, but he straightened up and his bomb aimer, Pilot Officer Chance—by a very good chance indeed—lobbed his "tallboy" a direct hit on the viaduct. There was one more direct hit and a lot of near misses. Two piers collapsed, another one was thrown 15 feet out of alignment and earthquake shock threw a span off another pier. Target destroyed.

Next day they went to the Nienburg Bridge, near Bremen, over which the Germans were taking oil to the front. It was not heavily defended, so Fauquier evolved a new plan to try and save some of the precious earthquake bombs. On the way up to the target he ordered four aircraft to start their bombing runs and told the others to circle near by and wait for orders in case the first four missed. It was an unprecedented idea, and the very fact that Fauquier considered it possible speaks eloquently of their phenomenal accuracy. He himself dived low to one side of the target to watch.

The results were fantastic. The four Lancasters made a steady run in loose formation and bombed almost in the same second. Fauquier saw the first two bombs hit simultaneously (one of them a "grand slam") on each end of the bridge. The bridge span lifted bodily and still intact into the air, seemed to hang there a second, and in that very moment a third bomb hit it fair and square in the middle. When the smoke had cleared there was no visible sign of the bridge whatsoever and the squadron turned for home, taking their fifteen remaining bombs with them.

Fauquier said when he landed, "I'd hate to have to do *that* again to prove it."

The Germans had one last railway bridge still serving the Ruhr; it was also near Bremen, and 617 went there early next morning. The first three bombs (from 16,000 feet) hit almost in the same second, all direct hits (including Fauquier's and Calder's "grand slams"). The next two were very near misses, followed by what seemed to be one more direct hit before smoke smothered the ruins.

As there were no worthwhile bridges left, 617 went back on the U-boat pens. At Farge, near Bremen, 7,000 slaves had sweated for two years to build the biggest concrete structure in the world, 1,450 feet long, over 300 feet wide and 75 feet high. The roof was 23 feet of solid reinforced concrete and the pens were just ready for use. 617 paid their call on March 27 and sank two "grand slams" deep in the roof which exploded right through, making holes 20 feet across and bringing down thousands of tons of concrete. Several "tallboys", direct hits and near misses, cracked the monster and undermined it and the pens were never used.

It was hard to find good targets now till a recce plane brought a report that Germany's last pocket battleship, the *Lutzow*, was sheltering in Swinemunde, in the Baltic. 617 slogged up there and sank her. Then they took some "grand slams" and "tallboys" to Heligoland and plastered half the island fortress's big guns. Next day they went back and plastered the other half, ending Germany's mastery of the approaches to the north-west ports.

Cochrane went to take over Transport Command, which, now the shooting was nearly over, was coming into its own. The new 5 Group A.O.C. told Fauquier he was grounded because he did not want him killed in the last moments. The tough Canadian had just finished his third tour and had won three D.S.O.s and a D.F.C.

The remnants of the Wehrmacht were said to be pulling back into Hitler's "Southern Redoubt" in Bavaria, where Berchtesgaden lay. It seemed that there was no more work for 617 till someone remembered that Hitler had recently told his Party chiefs, "I have read these days in the British Press that they intend to destroy my country house. I almost regret that this has not been done, for what I call my own is not more valuable than my compatriots possess."

Eager to ease his conscience, 617 flew to Berchtesgaden, hoping that if Hitler was there they might bury him in his house. As the world knows, Hitler was in Berlin, but it made no difference because the land was deep under snow and Berchtesgaden merged with the white hills and low cloud so that the squadron could not pick it out. However, they identified the near-by S.S. barracks, home of Hitler's body-guard, and flattened them with four "tallboys" and a selection of 1,000-pounders, and that, with Hitler away, was probably more useful than laying their eggs on the Eagle's Nest.

That was 617's last operation. On May 8 it was all over and the 150 pilots, navigators, bomb aimers, wireless operators, engineers and gunners realised they were going to have the same chance as ordinary people of walking down the years to a more natural death.

But no. Not quite. 617 and one other squadron were detailed for "Tiger Force", to be the R.A.F.'s contribution to the strategic bombing of Japan. They were to fly from Okinawa and drop their "tallboys" and "grand slams" on the bridges connecting Kyushu to the main Japanese island of Honshu to cut off reinforcements when the Americans invaded Kyushu, as they planned, in January, 1946. They were all set to go when the two bombs so much deadlier than "Grand Slam" fell on Hiroshima and Nagasaki and Japan surrendered.

"They must have heard we were coming," said the thwarted volunteers.

EPILOGUE

After the war, Wallis' friends urged him to claim a reward for his war-time inventions, but he said that if he did he would never touch such money for himself. I asked him why, and he said, "My dear chap, go and read your Bible. Turn up Samuel II, chapter twenty-three. You probably haven't got a Bible, so I'll tell you this story about David:

"He was hiding in the cave of Adullam after the Philistines had seized Bethlehem, and in his anguish he said, 'Oh that one would give me drink of the water of the well of Bethlehem, which is by the gate!' Now the three mighty men who were his lieutenants were with him, and I'm dashed if they didn't fight their way through the Philistine lines and draw a goatskin of water out of the well by the gate. They fought their way back and took the water to David in the cave, but when they told him how they had got it he would not drink it. They asked him why, and he said:

"'Is not this the blood of the men that went in jeopardy of their lives?'"

THE END

(*Just after this was written the Royal Commission on Awards to Inventors granted Barnes Wallis £10,000 for his wartime work. He immediately put it all into a fund to help educate the sons and daughters of men who died serving with the Royal Air Force.*)